JavaScript Essentials

Crafting Dynamic Web Experiences

David Brooks

Table of Contents

INTRODUCTION

"JavaScript Essentials: Crafting Dynamic Web Experiences" is a priceless manual designed to take novice and expert web developers alike on a life-changing exploration of the complex world of JavaScript. In the modern digital world, web applications are the ruler, and JavaScript is essential to creating dynamic and captivating online content. This book is like a lighthouse, showing readers the way to become proficient with JavaScript and giving them the courage to use its power.

The main goal of this book is to demystify JavaScript by dissecting difficult ideas into comprehensible sections that programmers of all skill levels can understand. All readers, from beginners looking to learn the basics to seasoned pros looking to hone their craft, will benefit from the methodical approach and thorough content found in these pages.

The first step of the journey is to explore the fundamentals of JavaScript, including variables, data types, control flow, and functions. With concise explanations and useful examples, readers will get a strong foundation in JavaScript that they can expand upon. The intricacy increases with each chapter, exploring more complicated subjects including error management, asynchronous programming, and DOM manipulation. In addition to understanding these ideas, readers will learn how to implement them successfully in their own projects through practical exercises and real-world scenarios.

Moreover, this book introduces readers to the newest capabilities included in ECMAScript 6 and later, acting as a portal to the world of contemporary JavaScript. Readers will learn the skills necessary to write code that is clearer and more effective, from arrow functions and template literals to destructuring assignments and spread operators.

But learning JavaScript is more than just memorizing its syntax and features; it's also about comprehending how it fits into the larger scheme of web development. As a result, this book also examines well-known frameworks and libraries, including React, Angular, and Vue.js, giving readers a comprehensive understanding of the ecosystem and enabling them to select the best resources for their projects.

Furthermore, "JavaScript Essentials" is a guide for both professional and personal development rather than merely a technical book. Readers will find motivation, support, and useful guidance to help them through the trials and successes of their journey as developers throughout these pages. This book will be your reliable guide every step of the way, whether your goal is to advance your profession, sharpen your skills, or just keep on top of the game.

"JavaScript Essentials: Crafting Dynamic Web Experiences" is essentially more than just a book; it's a catalyst for change, a doorway to new opportunities, and an evidence of the infinite ways that JavaScript may shape the web's future. So come along with us as we set out on this journey together, and let's explore JavaScript to the fullest, one page at a time.

CHAPTER I

Understanding JavaScript Basics

Introduction to JavaScript

The JavaScript programming language is a foundational language that has developed from its initial concept to become a vital tool for the development of dynamic and interactive web sites. It is considered the cornerstone of modern web development. Its rise from a basic scripting language intended to provide animation to online sites to a complete component of the web development trifecta, alongside HTML and CSS, highlights its significance in the modern era. This section explores the fundamentals of JavaScript, its features, and its vital role in web development, providing an understanding of why it has grown to be an essential competency for developers.

Netscape Communications first released JavaScript in 1995 with the goal of expanding the capabilities of web pages, which at the time were static and could only show text and images. JavaScript was created by Netscape programmer Brendan Eich in an astonishingly fast ten days. JavaScript is essentially unrelated to Java, despite the name implying otherwise. The name was chosen more as a marketing ploy than as a sign of technical descent. It is an interpreted language, which means that the web browser itself runs it line by line without the need for compilation. This feature, which enables scripts to run on the user's computer and dynamically alter content, is essential to its function in web pages.

JavaScript's ability to work with HTML and CSS, the building blocks of web pages, is what gives it its essential capability. JavaScript has the ability to work with HTML elements, modifying their appearance, attributes, and styles. With this feature, developers may make dynamic forms, animate elements, and react to keyboard inputs, clicks, and hovers from users. Additionally, the asynchronous nature of JavaScript—especially when combined with technologies like AJAX, or Asynchronous JavaScript and XML—allows web applications to interact with servers in the background and retrieve data without requiring a page reload. This has opened the door for the creation of sophisticated, responsive web applications with real-time user interfaces updates that resemble desktop applications.

The Document Object Model (DOM), a structured representation of the web page, is one of JavaScript's most important contributions to web development. JavaScript can access and dynamically modify the page's content, structure, and styles due to the Document Object Model (DOM). JavaScript's ability to work with the DOM is what makes it such an effective tool for developing dynamic and interactive user interfaces. In response to user interactions, developers have the ability to add, remove, or modify components and characteristics in ways that were not possible in the early days of the web.

The popularity of JavaScript in web development has increased even more with the introduction of frameworks and libraries like React, Angular, and Vue.js. These tools expedite the development process and promote the production of intricate, high-performing web applications by giving developers pre-written JavaScript code to accomplish basic tasks. In addition to increasing productivity, frameworks and libraries promote the use of web development best practices and patterns, which helps to produce systems that are more reliable, scalable, and maintainable.

With the release of Node.js, JavaScript's reach has extended to the server side in addition to its client-side capabilities. Developers can utilize Node.js, a JavaScript runtime built on top of Chrome's V8 JavaScript engine, to write server-side JavaScript code. Because of this, isomorphic JavaScript has emerged, which makes development easier and guarantees a smooth user experience by allowing the same code to operate on both the client and server sides. JavaScript is an even more attractive option for full-stack development due to its versatility, as it can handle both frontend and backend development.

It is impossible to exaggerate the significance of JavaScript in web development. It is an ability that is absolutely necessary for web developers because it is utilized in every web browser and plays a crucial part in the building of the front end of the website. Because of the language's versatility and the abundance of tools and resources available, one may create anything from basic webpages to intricate web applications. JavaScript's ongoing development, demonstrated by the frequent release of new features and enhancements, guarantees its applicability in the quickly evolving field of web technology.

In conclusion, the evolution of JavaScript from a simple scripting language to the foundation of interactive web development demonstrates its essential function in the digital age. Its versatility and strength are highlighted by its support for asynchronous programming, its ability to control the DOM, and its expansion into server-side development with Node.js. Its status as a vital tool for developers has been further cemented with the introduction of frameworks and libraries. JavaScript is becoming more and more important as the web develops, and any developer hoping to succeed in the field of web development needs to know this language.

Variables and data types

When it comes to programming, having a strong understanding of variables and data types is vital for properly manipulating data and producing software that is both effective and efficient. This is because both of these components are essential for the development of software. Through its variable declarations and a large variety of data types, JavaScript, which is a programming language that is both flexible and widely used, offers a comprehensive collection of capabilities for managing data resources. This section delves into the complexities of JavaScript's variables and data types, illuminating how these elements serve as the foundation for data manipulation within the language.

Data values can be stored in JavaScript variables, which are containers for storing data. They play an important part in programming because they enable developers to label data with names that are descriptive, which in turn makes the code more understandable and easier to maintain after it has been written. Declaring variables in JavaScript can be done in a number of different methods, each of which has its own scope and use case. Historically, the var keyword was utilized for the purpose of declaring variables, which may either provide function-scoped or globally-scoped variables depending on the context in which they were declared. On the other hand, let and const were added with the release of ECMAScript 2015 (ES6), which provided block-scoped alternatives to the var. Developers are able to declare variables that can be reassigned by using the let keyword. This helps them to accommodate situations in which the value of a variable is anticipated to change over the course of time. Const, on the other hand, is used to declare variables that are not intended to be reassigned. This indicates that the value of the variable is intended to remain constant during its entire lifecycle, which improves the clarity and predictability of the code.

The decision between var, let, and const is an important one since it has an effect on the scope, lifespan, and mutability of the variable. There is a possibility of problems with variable shadowing and accidental alterations occurring when function-scoped variables are declared with the var keyword. Within the function, these variables are accessible from any point in the application. While block-scoped variables that are declared with let and const are only available within the block in which they are specified, such as loops or conditional statements, they offer improved control over the visibility of variables and reduce the likelihood of issues that are caused by scope leakage.

Considering that JavaScript is a dynamically typed language, it is not necessary for variables to be declared with a particular data type, and the types of variables can change while the program is running. This flexibility makes rapid development and iteration possible, but it also necessitates a comprehensive understanding of JavaScript's data types in order to identify and eliminate errors that are connected to data types. The data types that are used in JavaScript can be generally classified into two categories: primitive types and object types. Among the primitive types are undefined, which stands for an uninitialized variable; null, which indicates the intentional absence of any object value; boolean, which can be either true or false; number, which stands for numeric values (JavaScript uses floating-point arithmetic for all of its numeric operations); string, which stands for textual data; and symbol, which was introduced in ES6 as a unique and immutable primitive value, primarily used as the key of an object's property.

The JavaScript programming language includes object types, which are collections of properties, in addition to these base kinds. When it comes to storing keyed collections and more complicated entities, objects are the way to go. When it comes to storing ordered collections of values, arrays, which are a form of object, are utilized. Functions are another type of object that are blocks of code that are designed to carry out a certain activity. In JavaScript, functions are took into account to be first- class citizens, which means that they can be kept in variables, supplied as arguments to other functions, and returned from functions.

The dynamic nature of JavaScript, in conjunction with the diversity of its data types, makes it possible to manipulate data structures in a flexible manner and to create sophisticated functionality. However, this freedom also brings up issues, such as implicit type coercion, which is when JavaScript automatically changes types in specific scenarios. This might result in unanticipated behaviors if it is not properly understood and handled. JavaScript includes techniques such as the strict equality operator (===) to compare both value and type, thereby assisting developers in avoiding unintentional type conversions. This feature helps JavaScript developers reduce concerns of this nature.

For any JavaScript developer, it is essential to have a strong understanding of variables and data types and to be able to use them effectively. Using variable declarations with var, let, and const in the appropriate manner can assist in controlling scope and mutability, which ultimately results in code that is cleaner and more predictable. In a similar vein, developers are able to design data structures that are both subtle and efficient when they have a comprehensive understanding of JavaScript's data types. These data types range from primitives such as string, number, and boolean to more complicated objects and arrays. A rigorous approach to type management is required in order to guarantee the dependability and maintainability of the code. JavaScript's dynamic nature, while enabling flexibility and power, necessitates this approach.

In conclusion, variables and data types are fundamental components of JavaScript programming. These components make it possible to store, manipulate, and display data in a variety of different ways. By gaining an understanding of these ideas, developers will be able to completely utilize the capabilities of JavaScript, which will allow them to create applications that are not only functional but also resilient and easy to maintain. To emphasize the significance of having a thorough understanding of the principles of variables and data types in JavaScript, both the tools and approaches for working with data will continue to develop with the language as it continues to undergo further development.

Operators and expressions

In the landscape of JavaScript programming, operators and expressions are the building blocks that allow developers to perform operations on variables and values, enabling decision-making, data manipulation, and complex logic implementation. This section delves into the intricacies of operators and expressions in JavaScript, highlighting their critical role in the language and how they facilitate the creation of dynamic and interactive web applications.

Operators in JavaScript are symbols or keywords that tell the interpreter to perform specific mathematical, relational, or logical operations and return a result. These operators are categorized into several types, including arithmetic, comparison, logical, assignment, bitwise, and special operators such as ternary operators. Each category is pivotal in data manipulation and decision-making processes within JavaScript code.

Arithmetic operators are among the most fundamental, allowing the execution of mathematical operations like addition (+), subtraction (-), multiplication (*), and division (/), along with more specialized operations such as modulus (%) for finding the remainder of a division and increment (++) and decrement (--) operators for adding or subtracting one from a variable, respectively. These operators are crucial for performing calculations, processing numerical data, and implementing algorithms that require mathematical operations.

Comparison operators, such as equal to (==), not equal to (!=), strictly equal to (===), strictly not equal to (!==), greater than (>), less than (<), greater than or equal to (>=), and less than or equal to (<=), are used to compare two values and return a boolean result (true or false). These operators are essential for control flow in scripts, allowing for the implementation of conditional statements that execute different code blocks based on the comparison outcome.

Logical operators, such as AND (&&), OR (||), and NOT (!), are used to combine multiple boolean expressions or values and return a single boolean outcome. These operators are pivotal in constructing complex conditional statements, enabling developers to implement sophisticated logic in their programs.

Assignment operators, including the basic assignment operator (=) and compound assignment operators like +=, -=, *=, and /=, are used to assign values to variables. Compound assignment operators provide a shorthand for updating the value of a variable based on its current value, facilitating more concise and readable code.

Bitwise operators, which operate on the binary representations of numbers, include AND (&), OR (|), NOT (~), XOR (^), left shift (<<), right shift (>>), and unsigned right shift (>>>). These operators are less commonly used in everyday web development but are invaluable for tasks that require low-level data manipulation, such as graphics programming and optimization of performance-critical code.

The ternary operator, a special operator represented by the syntax condition ? expression1 : expression2, provides a shortcut for the if-else statement, allowing developers to execute one of two expressions based on the truthiness of a given condition. This operator is particularly useful for making concise conditional assignments and decisions within expressions.

Expressions in JavaScript are combinations of values, variables, and operators that are evaluated to produce another value. Expressions enable developers to construct meaningful pieces of code that calculate values, perform operations, and determine the flow of execution within applications. JavaScript supports various types of expressions, including arithmetic expressions that perform mathematical calculations, string expressions that concatenate or manipulate strings, and logical expressions that evaluate to true or false based on the logical operators applied.

The interplay between operators and expressions is a fundamental aspect of JavaScript programming, enabling the dynamic and flexible data manipulation. Through expressions, developers can construct complex logic that responds to user interactions, processes data, and controls the execution flow in web applications. The diversity of JavaScript's operators, which range from the simplicity of arithmetic operators to the conditional logic of the ternary operator, offers developers a powerful toolkit that enables them to design web experiences that are rich, dynamic, and responsive.

In conclusion, operators and expressions are indispensable elements of JavaScript, providing the syntax and tools necessary for data manipulation, decision-making, and dynamic content generation. By mastering these concepts, developers can unlock the full potential of JavaScript, crafting applications that are not only functional but also intuitive and engaging. By ensuring that developers are able to continue to push the boundaries of what is possible in web development, it is essential that they have a solid understanding of operators and expressions and that they are able to use them effectively. JavaScript is continuing to improve and gain popularity.

Control flow (if statements, loops)

Control flow mechanisms in JavaScript, such as if statements and loops, are fundamental constructs that dictate the execution order of code blocks based on specific conditions or repeat them for a set number of times or until a particular condition is met. These constructs are vital for creating dynamic web applications that respond to user inputs, process data, and perform tasks in an efficient and logical manner. This section delves into the intricacies of control flow in JavaScript, focusing on the critical role of if statements and loops in facilitating decision-making and repetitive task execution within the language.

If statements are the cornerstone of conditional execution in JavaScript. They allow developers to specify blocks of code that should only be executed if a certain condition is true. The basic structure of an if statement has the keyword 'if', followed by a condition in parentheses and a code block enclosed in curly braces. If the condition evaluates to true, the code block is executed; otherwise, it is skipped. This simple yet powerful mechanism enables developers to introduce decision-making into their scripts, allowing for the dynamic generation of content, conditional processing of data, and handling of user interactions based on specific criteria.

For scenarios requiring more complex decision-making, JavaScript offers else and else if extensions to the basic if statement. The else clause can be used to execute an alternative block of code if the initial if condition is false.

The else if clause allows for the testing of multiple conditions in a sequence, where each condition is checked in turn, and the corresponding code block is executed for the first condition that evaluates to true. This chain of if-else if-else statements enables developers to handle multiple scenarios in a structured and readable manner, providing a clear path of execution for various conditions.

Loops, on the other hand, are control flow constructs that repeat a block of code as long as a specified condition remains true. JavaScript supports several types of loops, including for, while, and do-while, each serving different purposes and offering various ways to control the flow of repetition. The for loop is particularly useful for iterating over a fixed set of values or executing a code block a specific number of times. It consists of an initializer, a condition, and an increment expression, all enclosed within parentheses, providing a compact and flexible way to control the loop's behavior.

The while loop provides a more flexible structure for repetition, executing its code block as long as its condition evaluates to true. This loop is ideal for scenarios where the number of iterations is not known in advance, such as processing user inputs or reading data streams. The do-while loop is same with the while loop but ensures that code block is executed at least once before the condition is checked, making it suitable for situations where the initial execution of the loop body is required regardless of the condition's truth value.

Loops in JavaScript also support control statements such as break and continue, which provide additional control over the flow of repetition. The break statement immediately exits the loop, transferring control to the first statement following the loop. This is particularly useful for terminating the loop execution based on a condition other than the loop's own test condition. The continue statement, conversely, skips the remaining code in the current iteration and proceeds with the next iteration of the loop. This allows for the skipping of specific loop iterations based on conditional checks, enhancing the flexibility and efficiency of loop execution.

The combination of if statements and loops in JavaScript provides a robust framework for controlling the flow of execution in web applications. These constructs enable developers to implement complex logic, handle an array of user interactions, and process data dynamically and efficiently. By leveraging if statements, developers can direct the execution path of their scripts based on conditions, while loops allow for the performance of repetitive tasks without redundant code, streamlining the development process and enhancing the functionality and user experience of web applications.

In conclusion, control flow mechanisms such as if statements and loops are indispensable elements of JavaScript programming, enabling developers to create interactive, dynamic, and efficient web applications. By understanding and effectively utilizing these constructs, developers can introduce logic and structure into their code, allowing for conditional execution and repetitive task automation. As JavaScript continues to evolve as a key player in the web development landscape, the mastery of control flow constructs remains a crucial skill for developers, empowering them to build sophisticated and responsive web applications that meet the requirements of today's users.

Functions and scope

Functions in JavaScript play a pivotal role in structuring and organizing code, enabling developers to encapsulate blocks of logic that can be reused across different parts of an application. They not only contribute to cleaner and more maintainable code but also facilitate the creation of modular and scalable web applications. This section explores the concept of functions and scope in JavaScript, delving into the significance of these constructs and how they influence the behavior and structure of JavaScript programs.

Functions are defined blocks of code designed to perform a particular task or calculate and return a value. In JavaScript, functions can be created in various ways, including function declarations, function expressions, and arrow functions introduced in ES6 (ECMAScript 2015). A function declaration involves specifying the function keyword followed by a name, a list of parameters enclosed in parentheses, as well as the function body enclosed in curly braces. Function expressions allow the assignment of an anonymous function to a variable, offering more flexibility in how functions are defined and invoked. Arrow functions offer a more concise syntax for writing functions, using an arrow (=>) to separate the parameters from the function body, and are particularly useful for short functions and those that do not require their own this context.

The concept of scope is intrinsically linked to functions in JavaScript. Scope determines the accessibility of variables and functions in various parts of a program. JavaScript employs lexical scoping, meaning that the scope of a variable is described by its location within the source code and is constrained to the block or function in which it is declared. There are two main kinds/types of scope: global scope and local (or function) scope. Variables declared outside of any function are in the global scope as well as are accessible from anywhere in the code. Conversely, variables declared within a function are in the local scope of that function and cannot be accessed from outside the function.

This scoping mechanism is crucial for preventing variable name collisions and for managing memory efficiently. By limiting the lifespan and accessibility of variables to the context in which they are needed, JavaScript ensures that the global namespace is not polluted with unnecessary data, reducing the risk of naming conflicts and enhancing code modularity.

Closure is a powerful feature in JavaScript related to function scope. A closure occurs when a function is able to remember and access variables from its lexical scope, even when the function is executing outside that scope. This enables functions to have private variables and methods, making closures a key concept in JavaScript for information hiding and encapsulation. Through closures, developers can create factory functions, modules, and other constructs that rely on private state, contributing to the robustness and security of the code.

Furthermore, JavaScript's function scope plays a significant role in the hoisting mechanism. Hoisting is JavaScript's behavior of moving declarations (variables and functions) to the top of their scope prior code execution. This means that functions and variables can be used before they are declared in the code, provided they are declared in the same scope. Understanding hoisting is essential for developers to predict the behavior of their code accurately, especially when dealing with variable and function declarations.

The introduction of block scope in ES6 with the let and const keywords has further refined the control developers have over the scope. Unlike variables declared with var, which are function-scoped, let and const declare variables that are block-scoped, meaning they are confined to the block, statement, or expression in which they are declared. This addition allows for more precise scoping rules and helps prevent common errors related to variable hoisting and scope leakage.

In conclusion, functions and scope are fundamental aspects of JavaScript that significantly impact the structure, behavior, and security of code. Functions allow for the modularization of code, enabling developers to write reusable, maintainable blocks of logic. The concept of scope, along with closures and the distinction between global, local, and block scopes, provides a framework for controlling the visibility and lifetime of variables and functions. Together, these constructs empower developers to create complex, efficient, and scalable web applications. As JavaScript continues to evolve, understanding these core principles remains essential for anyone looking to master the language and leverage its full potential in web development.

CHAPTER II

Working with JavaScript Objects

Introduction to objects in JavaScript

In the vast and dynamic world of JavaScript programming, objects play a crucial role as one of the core data types that enable developers to store collections of data and more intricate entities. Unlike primitive data types such as numbers, strings, and booleans, objects in JavaScript offer a flexible structure for representing real- world entities in a way that is both intuitive and powerful. This section provides an introduction to objects in JavaScript, exploring their significance, structure, and the myriad ways in which they can be employed to enhance web development projects.

Objects in JavaScript are essentially collections of key-value pairs, where each key (also known as a property) is associated with a value that can be a primitive data type, another object, or a function. These key-value pairs provide a structured way to store data, allowing developers to model real-world entities such as users, products, and events in a way that is easily accessible and manipulatable within code. For example, an object representing a person might include properties for their name, age, and occupation, each associated with corresponding values that describe an individual.

Creating objects in JavaScript can be achieved in several ways. The most straightforward method is using object literals, which involve defining an object and its properties within curly braces. This approach is both concise and highly readable, making it a popular choice for defining simple objects. Additionally, JavaScript provides constructors and the new keyword for creating instances of objects based on predefined templates or classes, offering a more structured approach for object creation, especially when dealing with multiple instances of the same type of object.

One of the most powerful aspects of JavaScript objects is their ability to contain functions as values of properties, known as methods. Methods are known as the functions that are associated with an object and typically operate on the data contained within that object. By including methods in objects, developers can encapsulate behavior along with data, allowing for a more integrated and object-oriented approach to programming. This encapsulation not only makes code more modular and reusable but also facilitates the modeling of complex behaviors and interactions within the application's domain.

The flexibility of JavaScript objects extends to their dynamic nature. Properties are able to be added, modified, and/or deleted at runtime, allowing objects to be modified according to the needs of the application as it executes. This dynamic capability makes JavaScript objects incredibly versatile, enabling developers to adapt data structures on the fly and implement complex logic and data manipulations with relative ease.

In addition to their use as standalone entities, objects in JavaScript also form the foundation for some of the language's most important features and constructs. For example, objects serve as the basis for JavaScript's prototype-based inheritance, where objects can inherit properties and methods from other objects. This mechanism provides a powerful and flexible alternative to classical inheritance models, allowing for more dynamic and less hierarchical object compositions.

JavaScript's built-in objects, such as Array, Date, and Math, further showcase the utility and versatility of objects in the language. These built-in objects provide developers with a rich set of tools for performing common tasks, such as manipulating arrays, handling dates and times, and performing mathematical calculations. The extensive standard library of objects in JavaScript significantly reduces the amount of code developers need to write, speeding up the development process and enhancing productivity.

Objects also play a pivotal role in the interaction with the Document Object Model (DOM) in web development. The DOM is represented as a tree of objects, each corresponding to elements on a webpage. Through JavaScript, developers can manipulate these objects to dynamically change the content, structure, as well as style of web pages, enabling the creation of interactive and responsive user interfaces. This interaction between JavaScript objects and the DOM is fundamental to the dynamic nature of modern web applications, allowing for real-time updates and interactions without the need for page reloads.

In conclusion, objects in JavaScript are a potent and essential feature of the language that provide a structured and flexible way to represent and manipulate data. Their ability to encapsulate both data and behavior, combined with their dynamic nature and the extensive ecosystem of built-in objects, makes them a cornerstone of JavaScript programming. Whether modeling complex entities, encapsulating application logic, or interacting with the DOM, objects are integral to creating sophisticated, efficient, and interactive web applications. As JavaScript continues to evolve and grow in popularity, the role of objects in the language remains central, underscoring their importance in the toolkit of every web developer.

Creating and manipulating objects

Creating and manipulating objects in JavaScript is a fundamental aspect of the language that enables developers to model complex data structures and functionalities. JavaScript objects are versatile and dynamic, allowing for the encapsulation of data and behavior in a way that mimics real-world entities. This section explores the various techniques for creating and manipulating objects in JavaScript, highlighting their flexibility, utility, and the powerful paradigms they support in web development.

Objects in JavaScript can be created in several ways, each with its own use cases and benefits. The simplest and most direct method is the use of object literals, which involves defining an object and its properties within curly braces. This approach is highly readable and straightforward, making it ideal for creating single instances of objects with a fixed set of properties. For example, defining a person object with properties for name, age, and occupation can be done succinctly with object literals. This method is not only quick but also immediately intuitive for defining simple objects.

Beyond literals, JavaScript supports the creation of objects through constructor functions. Constructors are special functions designed to instantiate new objects according to a predefined template. When called with the new keyword, a constructor function creates a new object, binds this to the new object, and sets the object's prototype to the constructor's prototype, enabling inheritance. This pattern is particularly useful for creating multiple instances of an object with similar properties and methods, ensuring consistency across objects and encapsulating the logic for object creation.

With the introduction of ECMAScript 2015 (ES6), JavaScript introduced class syntax as a more intuitive and cleaner way to create objects and implement inheritance, building upon the existing prototype-based inheritance. The class syntax provides a declarative approach to defining constructor functions and prototypes, making the code easier to understand and maintain. Although syntactically different, classes in JavaScript are essentially syntactic sugar over the existing prototype- based inheritance, offering a more familiar paradigm for developers coming from class-based languages.

Once objects are created, JavaScript provides a plethora of ways to manipulate them, enabling developers to modify properties, add new properties, delete existing ones, and traverse objects to access their values. Properties of an object can be accessed and modified using dot notation or bracket notation, allowing for dynamic interaction with the object's data. This flexibility is crucial for developing interactive and dynamic applications where the state of objects can change in response to user inputs or external data.

Adding methods to objects allows for encapsulating behavior alongside data, making objects more than just data containers. Methods defined within an object can operate on the object's properties, providing a mechanism for interacting with and modifying the object's internal state. This encapsulation is a key principle of object-oriented programming, facilitating modularity and reuse.

JavaScript also supports advanced manipulation techniques, such as using the Object.defineProperty() method to add new properties to an object or modify existing ones with precise control over their characteristics, including enumerability, configurability, and writability. This method allows for fine-grained control over how properties behave, further extending the flexibility and power of JavaScript objects.

The Object.assign() method is another powerful tool for manipulating objects, enabling the shallow copying of properties from the source objects to target object. This method is particularly useful for merging objects, copying properties, or creating new objects with existing properties, contributing to the ease of object manipulation and data management in JavaScript applications.

For more complex manipulation and inspection of objects, JavaScript offers methods like Object.keys(), Object.values(), and Object.entries(), which return arrays containing an object's keys, values, or key-value pairs, respectively. These methods are invaluable for iterating over objects, transforming objects into arrays for easier manipulation, or performing operations on the properties of an object.

In conclusion, creating and manipulating objects in JavaScript is a core aspect of the language that provides developers with the tools to model complex data structures and behaviors. From simple object literals to constructor functions and the class syntax, JavaScript offers multiple paradigms for creating objects. The language's rich set of features for object manipulation, including property access, method definition, and advanced property control, empowers developers to build dynamic, efficient, and sophisticated web applications. As JavaScript continues to evolve, the fundamental principles of object creation and manipulation remain vital for harnessing the full potential of the language in web development.

Object-oriented programming concepts (encapsulation, inheritance, polymorphism)

Object-oriented programming (OOP) is a paradigm that organizes software design around data, or objects, rather than functions and logic. Objects can be defined as instances of classes, which can encapsulate data and the functions that operate on the data. JavaScript, traditionally known for its prototype-based model, supports object-oriented programming concepts including encapsulation, inheritance, and polymorphism. These concepts enable developers to create more modular, reusable, and maintainable code. This section delves into how these foundational OOP concepts are implemented and utilized in JavaScript, offering insight into their significance and application in modern web development.

Encapsulation is one of the core principles of OOP, referring to the bundling of data (or attributes) and methods (or functions) that operate on the data into single units, or objects. In JavaScript, encapsulation can be gained through the use of functions and closures, allowing for the creation of public and private members within an object. This mechanism enables developers to hide the internal state of an object and also expose only the necessary parts of the object to the outside world, thereby protecting the object from unintended modifications and promoting a more controlled interaction with the object's data. For instance, a function within an object can access its private variables and functions, while those private variables cannot be directly accessed from outside the function, ensuring a clear separation between the object's interface and its implementation.

Inheritance is another fundamental concept of OOP that permits a class to inherit properties and methods from another class. In JavaScript, inheritance is primarily achieved through the prototype chain. Every object in JavaScript has a property called prototype, where an object can inherit properties and methods from another object. The use of the new keyword creates a new object that inherits from the constructor function's prototype. This prototype-based inheritance model in JavaScript enables the creation of a hierarchy of objects, where child objects inherit from parent objects, allowing for property and method reuse and reducing redundancy in code. ES6 introduced the class syntax, which provides a more familiar and easier way to implement inheritance through the extends keyword, although it remains syntactic sugar over JavaScript's existing prototype-based inheritance.

Polymorphism, the ability of objects to process data differently depending on their class or data type, is a concept that allows for a more flexible and dynamic use of objects. In JavaScript, polymorphism can be achieved through prototype-based inheritance, where methods inherited from a parent object can be overridden in a child object. This permits objects of different types to be treated as objects of a common super type, enabling a single interface to represent different underlying forms of data. Polymorphism in JavaScript enables developers to write more general and flexible code that can work with objects of multiple types, providing a powerful tool for implementing complex functionalities and interactions in web applications.

The implementation of these OOP concepts in JavaScript provides a robust framework for establishing complex and scalable web applications. Encapsulation ensures that objects maintain control over their state and expose only what is necessary, promoting a clear and concise interface. Inheritance allows for the hierarchical organization of objects, enabling the reuse of properties and methods across objects and reducing code duplication. Polymorphism enhances flexibility and adaptability, allowing developers to write code that are able to work on objects of multiple types.

However, it's important to note that JavaScript's approach to OOP is quite unique compared to class-based languages. JavaScript's prototype-based model offers a more flexible and less rigid structure for object creation and inheritance, aligning with the dynamic nature of the language. This flexibility can lead to innovative patterns and paradigms not commonly found in traditional OOP languages, but it also requires a deep understanding of JavaScript's prototypes, closures, and the this keyword to effectively leverage OOP concepts.

In conclusion, object-oriented programming concepts such as encapsulation, inheritance, and polymorphism are significant in JavaScript development, offering a structured approach to designing and organizing code. By understanding and applying these concepts, developers can enhance the modularity, reusability, and maintainability of their code, contributing to the development of robust and efficient web applications. Despite the unique prototype-based nature of JavaScript, the language provides comprehensive support for OOP principles, allowing developers to harness the power of object-oriented design in the context of modern web development.

Working with arrays and array methods

Arrays in JavaScript are high-level, list-like objects used to store multiple values in a single variable. They are a fundamental aspect of the language, enabling developers to work with collections of data efficiently and effectively. This section explores the nature of arrays in JavaScript, focusing on their versatility, the array methods provided by JavaScript to manipulate these structures, and the impact these features have on web development.

An array can keep elements of any type, including numbers, strings, objects, and even other arrays, making them highly versatile for programming tasks. Arrays are ordered, meaning each element has a numeric position in the list, known as its index, which starts from zero. This order is crucial for accessing, modifying, and iterating over elements within the array. JavaScript arrays are dynamic, allowing elements to be added or removed, and their size to change during runtime, providing a flexible way to handle collections of data.

Creating arrays in JavaScript can be done using array literals, which are denoted by square brackets containing a comma-separated list of elements, or by using the Array constructor function. The literal notation is more concise and commonly used, whereas the constructor can be useful in certain situations, such as creating an array of a specific length without initially populating it with elements.

Once an array is created, JavaScript provides a plethora of methods to perform operations on arrays, such as adding or removing elements, searching, sorting, and traversing. These methods are built into the Array prototype, making them available on all array instances. They can broadly be categorized into mutator, accessor, and iteration methods.

Mutator methods modify the array directly. Examples include push() and pop(), which add as well as remove elements from the end of an array, respectively. Similarly, shift() and unshift() add and remove elements from the beginning of an array. These methods alter the original array and are essential for managing collections of data dynamically.

Accessor methods, on the other hand, do not modify the array but return some representation of the array. slice() returns a shallow copy of a part of an array, while concat() merges two or more arrays into a new array. These methods are invaluable for working with subsets of array data or combining multiple arrays without altering the original arrays.

Iteration methods allow for functional programming patterns, letting developers apply functions to elements in an array. Methods like forEach(), map(), filter(), reduce(), and find() are powerful tools for data manipulation and querying. forEach() executes a given function once for each array element, while map() creates a new array with the results of calling a given function on each element in the calling array. filter() establishes a new array with all elements that pass the test implemented by the given function, allowing for the extraction of specific elements based on criteria. Reduce() applies a function against an accumulator and also on each element in the array (from left to right) to minimize it to a single value, useful for summing values or combining data in various ways. Find() returns the value of the first element in the given array that satisfies the provided testing function, making it useful for locating specific items.

These iteration methods embrace the principles of functional programming, encouraging the writing of pure functions without side effects, which can lead to more predictable and bug-free code. Moreover, they make code more concise and readable, abstracting away the boilerplate code of loops and conditionals traditionally used for array manipulation.

JavaScript's array methods significantly enhance the language's capability to handle data collections, allowing for complex operations to be performed with minimal code. They support a wide range of programming tasks, from simple list processing to more complex data manipulation and transformation required in modern web applications. By leveraging these built-in methods, developers can implement sophisticated functionalities efficiently, such as searching for items, filtering data based on criteria, transforming data structures, and aggregating values.

In conclusion, arrays and their methods in JavaScript constitute a powerful set of features for working with collections of data. The ability to store, access, modify, and iterate over array elements with ease and flexibility makes arrays indispensable for JavaScript programming. The comprehensive suite of array methods provided by JavaScript enables developers to write clean, efficient, and expressive code, facilitating the manipulation of data in sophisticated ways. As web applications continue to evolve, requiring more complex data handling and user interactions, the role of arrays and their methods in JavaScript programming remains central, underscoring their importance in the development of dynamic and interactive web experiences.

CHAPTER III

DOM Manipulation

Introduction to the Document Object Model (DOM)

The Document Object Model (DOM) is known as a programming interface for web documents. It represents the page so that programs can change the document structure, style, and content. The DOM provides a representation of the document as a structured group of nodes as well as objects, possessing various properties and methods. JavaScript's interaction with the DOM enables dynamic content updates, making it a cornerstone of modern web development. This section provides an introduction to the DOM in JavaScript, highlighting its significance, structure, and the ways it enables interactive and dynamic web experiences.

At its core, the DOM is known as a cross-platform and language-independent interface that treats an XML and/or HTML document as a tree structure wherein each node represents a part of the document. This tree includes not just the HTML or XML tags but also the attributes and text within those tags, allowing for comprehensive manipulation of all aspects of a document. The DOM is designed to be accessible and manipulable via JavaScript, providing a bridge between the static content of a web page and the dynamic capabilities of JavaScript programming.

The significance of the DOM in web development cannot be overstated. Before the advent of the DOM, web pages were largely static, requiring a reload for any content update. The DOM's introduction heralded a new era of web development, enabling interactive and dynamic web applications. JavaScript's interaction with the DOM allows developers to respond to user actions, alter document content, structure, and styling on the fly, and manipulate elements based on data received from server-side scripts or APIs, all without the need for a page reload.

The structure of the DOM is hierarchical, starting from the document object, which represents the entire web page. From there, the document can be navigated using various properties and methods provided by the DOM API. For example, elements can be accessed by their ID, classes, types, or relative position in the document tree. This structure allows for precise targeting and manipulation of elements, enabling developers to create rich, user-interactive web pages.

Manipulating the DOM with JavaScript involves several key operations: accessing elements, changing their properties, modifying their styles, listening for and responding to events, and creating or removing elements. Accessing elements can be done using methods like getElementById(), getElementsByClassName(), or the more modern querySelector() and querySelectorAll(), which allow for CSS-like selection of elements. Once an element is accessed, its properties can be read or modified, enabling dynamic content updates. For instance, changing the text of an element can be as simple as updating its innerText or innerHTML property.

Styling can be dynamically changed by altering the style property of an element, allowing for animations, visibility changes, and aesthetic modifications based on user interactions or other conditions. Event listeners can be added to elements, making it possible to execute JavaScript code in response to user actions such as clicks, keyboard input, or mouse movements. This interactivity is a key component of modern web applications, providing users with immediate feedback and creating a seamless user experience.

Furthermore, the DOM allows for the creation of new elements and the removal or alteration of existing ones. Using methods like createElement(), appendChild(), or removeChild(), developers can dynamically alter the document's structure, adding complexity and interactivity to web pages. This capability is particularly useful for single-page applications (SPAs), where user interactions lead to significant changes in the content and structure of the page without reloading.

The DOM's event model facilitates complex event handling by allowing events to bubble up or be captured down the DOM tree, providing a powerful mechanism for handling user inputs and interactions. This model supports sophisticated event handling strategies, such as event delegation, which can improve performance and simplify event management in applications with many interactive elements.

In conclusion, the Document Object Model is an essential aspect of web development, serving as the bridge between static HTML documents and dynamic JavaScript applications. Its structured representation of web documents as a tree of objects accessible and manipulable via JavaScript has revolutionized how web applications are built, enabling dynamic content updates, interactivity, and a rich user experience. Understanding the DOM and its manipulation through JavaScript is fundamental for any web developer looking to create modern, interactive web applications. As web technologies continue to evolve, the principles of DOM manipulation remain a critical skill set, underscoring the enduring importance of the DOM in the development of the web.

Accessing and modifying DOM elements

Accessing and modifying the Document Object Model (DOM) elements is a foundational aspect of web development with JavaScript. The DOM offers a structured representation of the HTML document, enabling developers to programmatically interact with the webpage. Through DOM manipulation, developers can dynamically change the content, structure, and style of a webpage without needing to reload it. This capability is crucial for creating interactive, dynamic web applications that respond to user inputs and behaviors in real time. This section explores the methodologies for accessing and modifying DOM elements in JavaScript, emphasizing the techniques and their implications for web development.

Accessing DOM elements is the first step in DOM manipulation. JavaScript offers several methods to select and access elements within the DOM, each serving different use cases. The getElementById method is one of the simplest and most efficient ways to access an element, as it retrieves the element that matches a specific ID. Given that IDs are unique within a page, this method provides a direct reference to the required element. Similarly, getElementsByClassName and getElementsByTagName return live HTMLCollections of elements matching the specified class names or tag names, respectively. These methods enable developers to work with groups of elements sharing common attributes.

The introduction of querySelector and querySelectorAll methods has significantly enhanced the flexibility of DOM element selection. querySelector returns the first element that matches a certain CSS selector, while querySelectorAll returns a static NodeList of all elements matching the selector. These methods allow for complex selections using CSS syntax, making it easier to target elements based on their hierarchy, attributes, and relation to other elements. This advancement has streamlined the process of accessing elements, especially in complex DOM structures.

Once an element or a collection of elements is accessed, JavaScript provides numerous properties and methods to modify these elements. The innerHTML and textContent properties are commonly used to change the content of an element. innerHTML allows for the insertion of HTML content into an element, enabling developers to add nested elements along with text. textContent, on the other hand, provides a safer way to change just the text content, protecting against security risks associated with injecting HTML content directly.

Modifying the structure of the DOM is also a critical capability, allowing for dynamic content updates. Methods such as appendChild, insertBefore, removeChild, and replaceChild enable developers to add, move, remove, and replace elements within the DOM tree. These methods facilitate the creation of interactive user interfaces where elements are dynamically adjusted based on user interactions or other conditions, such as adding a list item to a list or replacing an image with another.

Styling elements is another aspect of DOM manipulation, allowing for dynamic changes to the appearance of elements. The style property of an element can be used to change its CSS properties directly from JavaScript. For example, changing the color, visibility, or position of elements can be achieved by modifying the respective CSS properties through the style object. This capability is essential for creating responsive and interactive designs that adapt to user actions and preferences.

Event handling is closely tied to accessing and modifying DOM elements, as it enables interactivity within web applications. JavaScript allows event listeners to be attached to elements using the addEventListener method. This method takes an event type and a callback function as arguments, allowing developers to define custom behavior that should occur when the event is triggered. Event listeners can be used to detect clicks, hover actions, keyboard inputs, and many other user interactions, making web applications responsive and interactive.

In conclusion, accessing and modifying DOM elements in JavaScript is considered as a fundamental skill for web developers, enabling the creation of dynamic, interactive web applications. The methods provided by JavaScript for selecting elements, such as getElementById, querySelector, and others, offer flexibility and precision in targeting elements within the DOM. Once elements are accessed, developers have a wide array of properties and methods at their disposal to modify content, structure, and styling, as well as to attach event listeners for handling user interactions. These capabilities allow developers to enhance user experiences by dynamically updating webpages in response to user inputs, making web applications more engaging and responsive. As web technologies continue to evolve, the principles of DOM manipulation remain essential, underscoring the importance of mastering these techniques in the development of modern web applications.

Event handling

Event handling in JavaScript is a critical concept that allows web developers to establish interactive and dynamic user experiences. It involves detecting user actions such as clicks, key presses, mouse movements, and touches, and executing specific code in response to these actions. This capability is foundational to modern web development, enabling the creation of responsive interfaces that react to user inputs. This section delves into the intricacies of event handling in JavaScript, exploring how events are managed, the methodologies for attaching event listeners, and the significance of events in interactive web applications.

At its core, event handling revolves around the concept of events, which are actions or events that happen in the system you are programming, typically the web browser. JavaScript, being an event-driven language, provides a powerful API for working with these events. Events can be anything from the user interacting with the browser to the browser itself executing certain tasks like loading a page. The process of responding to these events is facilitated by event listeners, which are functions that wait for a particular event to occur and execute a block of code when that event is detected.

The traditional approach to event handling in JavaScript involved the use of inline event handlers, where an event handler is directly specified as an attribute of an HTML element. For example, using the onclick attribute of a button element to run a JavaScript function when the button is clicked. However, this approach tightly couples the HTML structure with JavaScript logic, making the code harder to maintain and scale. It also poses potential security risks as it allows for the injection of malicious code.

The modern and more flexible approach to event handling uses the addEventListener method. This method allows developers to attach an event listener to an element without modifying the HTML code, promoting a clean separation of concerns between the structure of the webpage and its behavior. The addEventListener method takes at least two arguments: the type of event to listen for (e.g., 'click', 'keydown') and the callback function to execute when the event occurs. This method offers a more robust and secure way to handle events, supporting multiple event listeners for the same event on a single element, and offers greater control over the event listening process.

Event propagation is another important concept in JavaScript event handling. It refers to the order in which events are received on an element and its ancestors. There are two phases of event propagation: bubbling and capturing. In the bubbling phase, an event starts from the target element and bubbles up to the ancestors, while in the capturing phase, the event is captured down from the topmost ancestor to the target element. The addEventListener method allows developers to specify which phase they want the event listener to work in by providing a third argument, a boolean value indicating whether the listener should be executed during the capturing phase.

Event objects play a crucial role in event handling, providing contextual information about the event, including the type of event, the target element, as well as any keys pressed during keyboard events. These objects are automatically passed as an argument to the event listener callback function, allowing developers to access and manipulate event-specific data within their event handling logic. For instance, preventing the default action of an event, stopping the propagation of an event, or dynamically determining which element initiated the event.

Event delegation is a powerful pattern in event handling, particularly useful for managing events on multiple elements. Rather than attaching an event listener to each element individually, event delegation involves attaching a single event listener to a parent element and using the event object to determine which child element initiated the event. This technique is efficient for handling events on elements that are dynamically added to the document, reducing the memory footprint and improving performance, especially in complex web applications with numerous interactive elements.

In conclusion, event handling in JavaScript is a fundamental aspect of creating interactive and responsive web applications. It enables developers to listen for user actions and respond with appropriate functionality, enhancing the user experience. The evolution from inline event handlers to the use of addEventListener has provided a more maintainable, secure, and flexible way to manage events. Understanding event propagation, working with event objects, and leveraging event delegation are crucial for effective event handling. As web applications grow in complexity and interactivity, mastering event handling in JavaScript remains an essential skill for web developers, letting them to build sophisticated interfaces that engage and respond to users in meaningful ways.

Manipulating styles and classes

Manipulating styles and classes in JavaScript is an essential aspect of dynamic web development, enabling developers to alter the appearance and layout of web elements on the fly. This capability is crucial for creating interactive and responsive user interfaces that adjust according to user interactions, preferences, or conditions. This section explores the methodologies and significance of manipulating styles and classes through JavaScript, highlighting how these operations contribute to the enrichment of user experiences on the web.

At its foundation, the ability to manipulate styles and classes allows developers to programmatically change the CSS properties of HTML elements, thereby modifying their visual presentation without altering the underlying HTML structure. JavaScript interacts with the Document Object Model (or DOM) to achieve this, providing a bridge between the static content of a webpage and the dynamic capabilities of scripting.

To manipulate styles directly, JavaScript offers access to the style property of DOM elements. This property is an object that represents an element's style attribute, containing CSS properties in camelCase notation. Developers can modify these properties directly to change the appearance of an element. For instance, changing the color, size, or visibility of elements can be done by setting the respective CSS properties on the style object. This method is particularly useful for applying inline styles dynamically, such as highlighting a field in a form when input validation fails or animating elements in response to user actions.

While direct style manipulation is powerful for changing individual CSS properties, managing complex styles or multiple style changes can become cumbersome. To address this, developers often manipulate classes, which are predefined sets of styles defined in external CSS stylesheets. JavaScript provides methods such as classList.add(), classList.remove(), classList.toggle(), and classList.contains() to manage the classes of elements. These methods offer a more structured and maintainable approach to changing styles, allowing developers to define styles in CSS and programmatically apply or remove these styles by manipulating an element's class list.

The classList property is particularly useful for adding or removing multiple classes simultaneously, enabling more complex style changes with minimal code. The toggle method, for example, allows for the easy implementation of interactive elements, such as drop-down menus or accordions, by adding or removing a class based on the element's current state. This approach not only keeps the JavaScript and CSS code separate but also leverages the full power of CSS for styling, including transitions, animations, and media queries, thereby enhancing the efficiency and scalability of code.

Manipulating styles and classes in JavaScript also plays a vital part in creating responsive designs that adapt to different device sizes and orientations. By dynamically changing styles or applying different classes, developers can ensure that web applications provide an optimal user experience across various devices. This adaptability is key to modern web development, where users access content through a wide range of devices with differing capabilities and screen sizes.

Furthermore, JavaScript's style and class manipulation capabilities are essential for developing interactive applications that respond to user inputs in real-time. For instance, changing the layout or color scheme of a webpage based on user preferences or interactions can significantly enhance the user experience, making applications feel more intuitive and personalized. This level of interactivity and personalization is increasingly expected in modern web applications, underscoring the importance of these techniques in web development.

In addition to enhancing user experience, manipulating styles and classes through JavaScript also contributes to the accessibility of web applications. By dynamically changing styles, developers can provide visual cues or adjust layouts to improve readability and navigation for users with disabilities. This consideration is crucial for creating inclusive web applications that are accessible to a broader audience, including those relying on assistive technologies.

In conclusion, manipulating styles and classes in JavaScript is a powerful tool in the arsenal of web developers, enabling the dynamic alteration of web elements' appearance and layout. Through direct manipulation of styles and structured management of classes, developers can create responsive, interactive, and accessible web applications that engage users and adapt to their needs. These techniques contribute significantly to the richness of web interfaces, offering a blend of aesthetics, functionality, and user experience that is fundamental to the success of modern web applications. As web technologies continue to evolve, the ability to manipulate styles and classes remains a key skill for developers, driving innovation and creativity in web design and development.

CHAPTER IV

Asynchronous JavaScript

Introduction to asynchronous programming

Asynchronous programming in JavaScript is a paradigm that allows for non-blocking operations, enabling web applications to remain responsive while performing tasks such as data fetching, file reading, or executing time-consuming computations. This programming style is crucial for developing efficient, fast, and user-friendly web applications. Traditional synchronous programming can lead to blocking behavior, where the browser becomes unresponsive until a task completes. Asynchronous programming addresses this issue by allowing tasks to run in the background and notifying the main thread upon completion. This section provides an introduction to asynchronous programming in JavaScript, exploring its significance, mechanisms, and the impact it has had on web development.

JavaScript, being single-threaded, relies on asynchronous programming to manage operations that could block the main thread and degrade the user experience. The evolution of asynchronous programming in JavaScript has seen the adoption of several patterns and features, including callbacks, promises, and async/await syntax, each improving upon the last in terms of readability, manageability, and ease of use.

Callbacks were the initial approach to handling asynchronous operations in JavaScript. A callback is known as a function passed as an argument to another function, which is then invoked inside the outer function to complete some type of routine or action. While callbacks are straightforward and effective for handling simple asynchronous tasks, they can lead to complex and hard-to-maintain code structures known as "callback hell" or "pyramid of doom," especially when dealing with multiple nested callbacks.

To address the shortcomings of callbacks, JavaScript introduced promises, representing the eventual completion (or failure) of an asynchronous operation and its resulting value. A promise in JavaScript is an object that encapsulates the state of an asynchronous operation, offering a cleaner, more powerful way to handle asynchronous tasks and their results. Promises support chaining, allowing developers to perform a sequence of asynchronous operations in a more readable and manageable way. With methods like then for success scenarios, catch for error handling, and finally for cleanup actions, promises provide a structured approach to asynchronous programming.

Building upon promises, the async/await syntax was introduced in ECMAScript 2017, further simplifying asynchronous programming in JavaScript. An async function returns a promise and allows the utilization of the await keyword to pause the function's execution until the promise settles. This syntax makes asynchronous code look and behave more like traditional synchronous code, improving readability and reducing the complexity associated with managing asynchronous operations.

Asynchronous programming in JavaScript is not only about managing operations that take time to complete but also about improving the overall performance and responsiveness of web applications. By leveraging asynchronous patterns, developers can ensure that web applications remain responsive, providing a smooth user experience. For instance, when fetching data from a server, reading files, or executing tasks that might take time, asynchronous programming allows these operations to occur in the background, with the user interface remaining interactive.

Moreover, asynchronous programming plays a crucial role in modern JavaScript development practices and frameworks. Many of JavaScript's APIs and libraries, such as Fetch API for network requests, are designed with asynchronous operations in mind. Frameworks and libraries like Node.js leverage asynchronous programming to handle I/O-bound tasks efficiently, making it possible to develop scalable network applications.

One of the significant impacts of asynchronous programming in JavaScript has been the facilitation of single-page applications (SPAs). SPAs rely heavily on asynchronous operations to fetch, display, and update data without requiring page reloads, providing a seamless and dynamic user experience akin to desktop applications. This model has transformed the way developers build web applications, emphasizing the importance of asynchronous programming in modern web development.

In conclusion, asynchronous programming in JavaScript is a fundamental concept that has dramatically influenced web development. Through the use of callbacks, promises, and the async/await syntax, JavaScript allows developers to write clean, efficient, and non-blocking code, enhancing the performance and user experience of web applications. As web technologies continue to evolve, the principles of asynchronous programming remain at the heart of creating responsive, interactive, and scalable web applications. Understanding and effectively utilizing asynchronous programming is essential for any web developer looking to build modern web applications that meet the needs of today's users.

Callback functions

Callback functions are a foundational concept in asynchronous JavaScript programming, allowing developers to handle operations that take an indeterminate amount of time to complete, such as data fetching, file reading, or any task that relies on external resources. These functions represent a powerful programming paradigm, enabling web applications to run time-consuming tasks in the background while maintaining a responsive user interface. This section delves into the role of callback functions in asynchronous JavaScript, exploring their significance, how they operate, and the impact they have on the development of dynamic web applications.

At its core, a callback function is known as a function passed into another function as an argument, which is then invoked inside the outer function to complete some kind of action. In the context of asynchronous operations, callback functions are used to specify what should happen once an asynchronous operation completes. This mechanism is crucial for JavaScript's single-threaded environment, where executing lengthy tasks synchronously would block the thread, leading to unresponsive interfaces and a poor user experience.

The significance of callback functions in asynchronous JavaScript cannot be overstated. They provide a means to ensure that certain code only runs after a preceding task has finished, a necessity in web development where operations often depend on data from network requests, user inputs, or other sources that are not immediately available. Callbacks enable developers to write non-blocking code, a fundamental aspect of creating smooth, user-centric web applications.

Callback functions operate by being passed to and executed by another function, typically one that performs an asynchronous operation. For example, when making an API request, a callback function can be passed to handle the response. The JavaScript runtime environment ensures that the callback is called at the appropriate time, allowing the main thread to continue executing other tasks in the meantime. This approach to asynchronous programming is known as "callback-based" or "continuation-passing style," where the continuation of the program's logic is encapsulated within callback functions.

Despite their utility, callback functions come with challenges, particularly when managing complex asynchronous operations. The most notable issue is "callback hell" or "pyramid of doom," a situation where callbacks are nested within callbacks, leading to deeply indented and hard-to-read code. This complexity arises from the sequential nature of some asynchronous operations, where one task must complete before another begins, requiring nested callbacks to manage the dependencies. The resulting code can be challenging to understand, maintain, and debug, highlighting the need for patterns and practices that can mitigate these challenges.

To address the complexities associated with callback functions, developers have adopted several strategies. Naming callbacks and modularizing code by breaking down operations into smaller functions can improve readability and maintainability. Furthermore, JavaScript has evolved to offer alternative patterns for managing asynchronous operations, such as Promises and the async/await syntax, which provide more elegant solutions to the callback hell problem. Nevertheless, understanding and effectively using callback functions remains essential, as they underpin these more advanced features.

The impact of callback functions on web development is profound. They have enabled the creation of highly interactive and responsive web applications by allowing for non-blocking operations. Before the widespread adoption of callbacks and asynchronous programming patterns, web pages were static and required reloading to update content. With callbacks, developers can create applications that update in real time, responding to the interactions of the user without the need for page refreshes. This capability has transformed the web into a platform for sophisticated applications, ranging from real- time chat applications to dynamic content management systems and interactive games.

In conclusion, callback functions play a critical role in asynchronous JavaScript, providing the means to perform non-blocking operations and enhance the interactivity and responsiveness of web applications. While they present challenges, particularly in managing complex or deeply nested asynchronous operations, their significance in modern web development cannot be understated. Callbacks have paved the way for the advanced asynchronous programming patterns that are now prevalent in JavaScript development, underscoring their foundational place in the language. As web technologies continue to advance, the principles of asynchronous programming, with callback functions at their core, remain vital for developers seeking to build fast, efficient, and user-friendly web applications.

Promises and async/await

In the landscape of modern web development, the introduction of Promises and the async/await syntax has significantly refined how asynchronous operations are handled in JavaScript. These features address the complexities and limitations of traditional callback-based approaches, providing a more intuitive and powerful way to work with asynchronous code. This section explores the concepts of Promises and async/await in asynchronous

JavaScript, detailing their functionality, advantages, and the transformative impact they have on writing clean, readable, and efficient code.

Promises represent a major advancement in asynchronous programming in JavaScript. A Promise is an object that encapsulates the eventual completion or failure of an asynchronous operation as well as its resulting value. It fundamentally changes the way asynchronous tasks are managed, moving away from the callback hell problem, characterized by nested callbacks and difficult-to-maintain code, to a more manageable and composable structure. At their core, Promises provide a more declarative approach to asynchronous programming, allowing developers to express what they want to do with the value returned from an asynchronous operation once it's available, or how they want to handle errors should they occur.

The essence of a Promise is that it can exist in one of three states: pending, fulfilled, and/or rejected. When a Promise is established, it is in the pending state, representing an ongoing operation. Upon successful completion of the operation, the Promise transitions to the fulfilled state, and in case of an error, it moves to the rejected state. Developers can attach callbacks to handle each of these outcomes using the then method for fulfillment and the catch method for rejection. This setup not only simplifies error handling by providing a clear mechanism for catching and dealing with errors but also allows for chaining multiple asynchronous operations in a way that is both readable and maintainable.

Building on the foundation laid by Promises, the async/await syntax introduced in ECMAScript 2017 has further streamlined asynchronous programming in JavaScript. The async keyword is employed to declare a function as asynchronous, indicating that it will return a Promise. Within an async function, the await keyword is used before an expression that returns a Promise. This pauses the execution of the async function until the Promise is resolved, at which point the async function resumes execution and returns the resolved value. The beauty of async/await lies in its ability to make asynchronous code look and behave more like traditional synchronous code, enhancing readability and simplifying the logic involved in handling asynchronous operations.

One of the key advantages of using Promises and async/await is improved error handling. Traditional callback-based approaches often led to complicated error handling logic, especially when dealing with multiple nested callbacks. With Promises, errors propagate down the chain of then calls until they are caught by a catch block, allowing for centralized error handling. This mechanism is further simplified with async/await, where a try/catch block can be used to wrap asynchronous operations, providing a familiar and straightforward way to handle both synchronous and asynchronous errors.

The introduction of Promises and async/await has had a transformative impact on web development. These features enable developers to write asynchronous code that is not only more readable and easier to understand but also more robust and easier to debug. The ability to chain Promises and the syntactic sugar provided by async/await reduce the complexity associated with managing multiple dependent or independent asynchronous operations. This leads to cleaner codebases, where the logic flow of asynchronous operations is more apparent, reducing the cognitive load on developers and enhancing maintainability.

Moreover, Promises and async/await facilitate the development of more responsive and interactive web applications. By allowing for non-blocking execution of asynchronous tasks, these features ensure that web applications remain responsive to user input, improving the general user experience. Whether fetching data from a server, processing files, or performing computationally intensive tasks, Promises and async/await enable these operations to be performed efficiently in the background, while not interrupting the user interface.

In conclusion, Promises and the async/await syntax represent significant advancements in asynchronous programming in JavaScript. By providing a more intuitive and powerful way to handle asynchronous operations, these features have greatly improved the readability, maintainability, and robustness of JavaScript code. They have addressed the challenges of callback-based programming, offering developers a more declarative approach to managing asynchronous tasks. As the intricacy of web applications continues to grow, the importance of understanding and leveraging Promises and async/await becomes increasingly critical for developers looking to build modern, efficient, and user-friendly web applications.

Handling asynchronous operations (AJAX requests, timeouts)

Handling asynchronous operations, such as AJAX requests and timeouts, is a cornerstone of modern web development, enabling the creation of dynamic, responsive, and interactive web applications. Asynchronous JavaScript as well as XML (AJAX) allows web pages to be updated asynchronously by exchanging little amounts of data with the server behind the scenes. This means that it is possible to update parts of a web page, without reloading the whole page, creating a seamless user experience. Timeouts, on the other hand, provide a way to execute code after a specified period, enabling delays, animations, or the deferment of operations until a later time. This section explores the intricacies of handling asynchronous operations in

JavaScript, focusing on AJAX requests and timeouts, their significance, and the methodologies employed to manage them effectively.

AJAX requests are fundamental to asynchronous web development, allowing data to be fetched from a server without the need for a full page refresh. This is achieved through the XMLHttpRequest object or more modernly through the Fetch API, which provides a more powerful and flexible interface for fetching resources. The process involves making a request to a URL and handling the response within the same page, thereby enhancing the application's interactivity and speed. This capability has been instrumental in the development of single-page applications (SPAs) where user actions trigger AJAX requests that fetch data or partial content, updating the user interface in real-time.

The traditional way to perform AJAX requests involved the XMLHttpRequest object. Developers would create an instance of this object, configure the request by specifying the method and URL, and define a callback function to handle the response. The request would then be sent, and the callback function executed once the response was received, allowing the application to process and display the fetched data accordingly. However, this approach often led to complex callback structures, especially when dealing with multiple dependent AJAX requests.

The introduction of Promises and the Fetch API has significantly simplified the handling of AJAX requests in JavaScript. The Fetch API returns a Promise, providing a cleaner and more readable way to make HTTP requests and process responses. Developers can use the then method to handle the response once it is available, and the catch method to handle any errors that happen during the request. This approach not only simplifies error handling but also supports the chaining of requests, making it easier to perform multiple, sequential AJAX calls with less code and complexity.

Timeouts in JavaScript are handled using the setTimeout and setInterval functions. setTimeout allows developers to specify code to be executed once after a delay, while setInterval executes code repeatedly at specified intervals. These functions are essential for adding delays, creating animations, or deferring the execution of code until a particular condition is met. For example, setTimeout can be used to delay the execution of a function, giving the illusion of asynchronous behavior even for operations that are inherently synchronous.

Handling timeouts effectively requires careful consideration, especially regarding the user experience. Excessive or unnecessary delays can frustrate users, while well-timed timeouts can enhance interactivity and responsiveness. For instance, debouncing and throttling techniques often rely on timeouts to optimize the performance of event handlers that are triggered frequently, such as during window resizing or keypress events. These techniques ensure that the code executes at a controlled rate, improving the application's efficiency and responsiveness.

The combination of AJAX requests and timeouts has enabled the development of sophisticated web applications that respond intelligently to user inputs and environmental changes. Real-time form validation, auto-saving features, and dynamic content loading are just a few examples of functionalities made possible through the effective handling of asynchronous operations in JavaScript. These capabilities have transformed the web from a collection of static pages into a platform for complex, application-like experiences.

In conclusion, handling asynchronous operations such as AJAX requests and timeouts is crucial for modern web development. These operations enable the creation of dynamic, efficient, and user-friendly web applications that operate seamlessly, providing instant feedback and interaction without the need for page reloads. The evolution of JavaScript, particularly with the advent of Promises, the Fetch API, and improved timeout management, has greatly simplified the development process. It has allowed developers to write cleaner, more maintainable code while leveraging the full potential of asynchronous operations. As web technologies continue to advance, the importance of mastering asynchronous operations in JavaScript remains paramount for developers aiming to build responsive, interactive, and engaging web applications.

CHAPTER V

Error Handling and Debugging

Understanding JavaScript errors

Understanding JavaScript errors is essential for any developer working within the web ecosystem. Errors in JavaScript can arise from various sources, including syntax mistakes, type errors, runtime exceptions, and logical errors in code. These errors can halt execution, lead to unexpected behavior, or even compromise the security and performance of web applications. A deep understanding of JavaScript errors, their types, handling mechanisms, and debugging strategies is crucial for developing robust, efficient, and secure web applications. This section explores the landscape of JavaScript errors, focusing on their nature, categorization, handling techniques, and the importance of effective error management in the development process.

JavaScript, being a dynamically typed and interpreted language, is prone to a variety of errors. Syntax errors are the most basic form, occurring when the code deviates from the language's grammar rules. These are typically caught by JavaScript engines during the parsing phase prior the code is executed. Syntax errors are often the result of typos, missing tokens (such as brackets, commas, or semicolons), or misuse of language constructs. They are relatively straightforward to fix once identified, but they can prevent scripts from running entirely until corrected.

Runtime errors, or exceptions, occur while the code is executing. They can be caused by various issues, including attempting to call a non-existent function, accessing undefined variables, or violating the language's runtime rules, such as performing an illegal operation (e.g., dividing by zero). Unlike syntax errors, runtime errors may occur under certain conditions that are not always predictable at the parsing stage. This makes them more challenging to detect and handle, as they depend on the application's state and the data it processes at runtime.

Type errors are a subset of runtime errors that occur when an operation is performed on a value of an inappropriate type, such as trying to invoke a method on a non-function or accessing properties of null or undefined. Given JavaScript's loose typing system, type errors are common and can lead to subtle bugs if not properly managed. The language's coercion rules, which automatically convert values between different types under certain operations, can further complicate the detection and handling of type errors.

Logical errors represent mistakes in the implementation logic of a program, where the code does not perform as intended. These errors are often the most difficult to debug, as they do not necessarily result in thrown exceptions or immediately noticeable issues. Instead, they manifest as incorrect behavior or output, requiring careful analysis and understanding of the program's intended functionality to identify and resolve.

Handling errors effectively is a critical aspect of JavaScript programming. The language provides mechanisms such as try...catch blocks to gracefully catch and manage exceptions, allowing developers to maintain control over the program flow even when errors occur. The try block encloses code that may throw an exception, while the catch block specifies how to respond to the error, preventing it from propagating further and potentially crashing the application. Additionally, the finally clause can be used to execute code regardless of whether an error was thrown or caught, useful for cleanup operations.

For asynchronous code, error handling can be more complex due to the non-linear execution flow. Promises and async/await syntax offer structured ways to catch errors in asynchronous operations. Promises use the .catch() method to handle rejected cases, while async/await allows the use of traditional try...catch blocks to handle errors in an asynchronous context, improving readability and error management in asynchronous JavaScript code.

Debugging strategies for JavaScript errors involve a combination of tools and techniques. Developer tools available in modern browsers provide powerful debugging capabilities, including breakpoints, step execution, and call stack inspection, allowing developers to pause code execution and examine the variables and execution context at various points. Additionally, logging can be an effective way to track the application's state and identify the circumstances leading up to an error.

Understanding and managing JavaScript errors is fundamental to the development of reliable and resilient web applications. By comprehensively grasping the types of errors that can occur, employing effective error handling mechanisms, and utilizing debugging tools and strategies, developers can mitigate the impact of errors on the user experience and application stability. Moreover, a proactive approach to error management, including thorough testing and the use of static analysis tools, can help prevent many common errors from occurring in the first place. As JavaScript continues to evolve and its use in complex web applications grows, the importance of mastering error handling and debugging techniques becomes ever more critical for developers aiming to build high-quality, robust web solutions.

Debugging techniques (console.log, breakpoints, browser developer tools)

Debugging techniques are essential tools in a developer's arsenal, especially when working with JavaScript, a language known for its dynamic nature and potential for errors. Effective debugging allows developers to identify and resolve issues in their code, leading to more reliable and efficient web applications. This section explores various debugging techniques in JavaScript, including console.log statements, breakpoints, and browser developer tools, highlighting their significance and how they are used to diagnose and fix problems in JavaScript code.

Console.log statements are one of the simplest yet most powerful debugging tools in JavaScript. They allow developers to print messages or values to the browser's console, providing insight into the state of the application at different points in time. Console.log statements are commonly used to log variable values, function calls, or the execution flow of the code. By strategically placing console.log statements throughout the code, developers can gain visibility into the program's behavior and track the values of variables as the code executes. This technique is specifically useful for identifying unexpected behavior or pinpointing the source of errors in complex codebases.

Breakpoints are another essential debugging technique in JavaScript, allowing developers to pause the execution of code at specific points and inspect the program's state. Breakpoints can be set directly in the browser's developer tools or through the code editor's debugger interface. Once a breakpoint is triggered, the execution of the code halts, and developers can examine the call stack, inspect variables, and step through the code line by line. This interactive debugging approach provides a granular view of the code's behavior and allows developers to identify and fix issues with precision.

Browser developer tools, such as those provided by Chrome, Firefox, and Edge, offer a comprehensive suite of debugging features for JavaScript development. These tools include a variety of panels and functionalities, such as the Elements panel for inspecting and modifying the HTML and CSS of the page, the Console panel for logging messages and executing JavaScript code, and the Sources panel for debugging JavaScript code directly within the browser. The debugger interface within the Sources panel allows developers to set breakpoints, step through code, and analyze variables, providing a powerful environment for debugging complex JavaScript applications.

In addition to breakpoints and console.log statements, browser developer tools offer a range of advanced debugging features, including network monitoring, performance profiling, and memory analysis. These features enable developers to identify performance bottlenecks, optimize code, and diagnose memory leaks, ensuring that web applications are both fast and efficient. Furthermore, browser developer tools are continuously evolving, with new features and improvements added regularly to support the ever-changing landscape of web development.

Beyond traditional debugging techniques, modern JavaScript development also benefits from the utilization of static analysis tools and linters, which can help catch errors and enforce coding standards before the code is executed. Tools like ESLint, JSHint, and TypeScript provide static analysis of JavaScript code, flagging potential issues and enforcing best practices. Integrating these tools into the development workflow can help prevent common errors and ensure code quality from the outset.

In conclusion, debugging techniques play a vital role in JavaScript development, enabling developers to identify, diagnose, and fix issues in their code effectively. Console.log statements, breakpoints, and browser developer tools provide powerful mechanisms for gaining insight into the behavior of JavaScript applications and tracking down bugs. By mastering these debugging techniques and incorporating them into their workflow, developers can streamline the development process, improve code quality, and deliver more reliable and efficient web applications. As JavaScript continues to evolve and the complexity of web applications increases, the importance of effective debugging techniques becomes ever more crucial for developers striving to build high-quality software.

Error handling strategies

Error handling is a critical aspect of JavaScript programming, enabling developers to anticipate, manage, and recover from unexpected situations that may arise during code execution. Effective error handling strategies not only help ensure the reliability and stability of web applications but also contribute to a better user experience by gracefully handling errors and providing informative feedback to users. This section explores various error handling strategies in JavaScript, including try...catch blocks, error objects, and error logging, highlighting their significance and best practices for implementing robust error handling in JavaScript applications.

One of the primary mechanisms for error handling in JavaScript is the use of try...catch blocks. This construct allows developers to wrap code that may potentially throw an error within a try block and specify how to handle any resulting errors in a catch block. When an error happens within the try block, control is transferred to the corresponding catch block, where developers can implement custom error handling logic, including logging the error, displaying a user-friendly message, or gracefully degrading functionality. By encapsulating potentially problematic code within try...catch blocks, developers can prevent errors from propagating up the call stack and crashing the application, leading to a more robust and resilient codebase.

Error objects are another key component of error handling in JavaScript. When an error occurs, JavaScript generates an error object that contains information about the error, including its type, message, and stack trace. Error objects provide valuable context for understanding the nature and source of errors, helping developers diagnose and troubleshoot issues more effectively. By inspecting error objects within catch blocks or logging them to the console, developers can gain insights into the underlying cause of errors and take appropriate action to address them. Additionally, JavaScript provides built-in error types, such as SyntaxError, TypeError, and RangeError, which developers can use to distinguish between different types of errors and implement targeted error handling strategies.

Logging errors is a crucial aspect of error handling in JavaScript, allowing developers to record information about errors for diagnostic purposes. Console.log statements are commonly used to log error messages, stack traces, and other relevant information to the browser's console during development. However, in production environments, it is advisable to use more robust error logging solutions, such as server-side logging libraries or third-party error monitoring services. These tools capture errors occurring in production environments, aggregate them, and provide actionable insights to developers, enabling them to determine and address issues proactively. By logging errors systematically, developers can gain visibility into the health as well as performance of their applications and continuously improve their error handling strategies over time.

In addition to try...catch blocks, error objects, and error logging, JavaScript developers can leverage other techniques to enhance error handling in their applications. For example, defensive programming practices, such as input validation and defensive coding, can help prevent errors from occurring in the first place by checking for invalid inputs, handling edge cases, and using defensive constructs, such as guard clauses and null coalescing operators. Moreover, adopting a mindset of resilience and embracing failure as a natural part of software development can empower developers to design more fault-tolerant systems that gracefully handle errors and degrade gracefully under adverse conditions.

In conclusion, error handling is a fundamental aspect of JavaScript programming, enabling developers to anticipate, manage, and recover from errors gracefully. By using try...catch blocks, error objects, and error logging, developers can implement robust error handling strategies that improve the reliability and stability of their applications. Additionally, by adopting defensive programming practices and embracing failure as a natural part of software development, developers can design more resilient systems that gracefully handle errors and offer a better user experience. As JavaScript continues to evolve and the complexity of web applications increases, mastering effective error handling techniques becomes increasingly important for developers striving to build high-quality, reliable, and user-friendly software.

CHAPTER VI

ES6 and Beyond

Overview of ECMAScript 6 (ES6) features

ECMAScript 6 (ES6), also known as ECMAScript 2015, marked an important milestone in the evolution of the JavaScript language, introducing a wide range of new features, syntax enhancements, and improvements to the language. ES6 was the largest update to the JavaScript language since the release of ES5 in 2009, and its features have since become integral parts of modern JavaScript development. One of the most notable features introduced in ES6 is the addition of let and const keywords for declaring variables. These keywords provide block- scoped variable declarations, replacing the traditional var keyword, which has function-level scope. The introduction of let and const improves code clarity and predictability by preventing unintended variable hoisting and reducing the risk of variable reassignment.

Another significant addition to ES6 is arrow functions, which provide a concise syntax for defining anonymous functions using the => arrow syntax. Arrow functions provide several advantages over traditional function expressions, including implicit return statements, lexical scoping of this, and shorter syntax for simple one-liner functions. Arrow functions are widely used in modern JavaScript development for their readability, brevity, and compatibility with functional programming paradigms.

ES6 also introduced template literals, a new syntax for creating multi-line strings and interpolating variables and expressions within strings using backticks (`). Template literals offer a more expressive and flexible alternative to traditional string concatenation and interpolation, allowing developers to create complex strings more easily and intuitively.

Another key feature of ES6 is the spread operator (...), which allows for the expansion of iterable objects such as arrays or strings into individual elements. The spread operator is commonly used for array manipulation, object spreading, and function arguments, providing a more concise and expressive syntax for working with collections and iterable objects.

Additionally, ES6 introduced destructuring assignments, a powerful feature that allows for the extraction of values from arrays and objects into individual variables using syntax that mirrors the structure of the data being destructured. Destructuring assignments simplify the process of working with complex data structures, enabling developers to extract values more efficiently and intuitively.

ES6 also introduced classes and inheritance syntax, providing a more familiar and intuitive syntax for defining and working with object-oriented programming concepts in JavaScript. The class syntax in ES6 is based on prototypal inheritance but offers a more familiar syntax for developers coming from other object-oriented languages such as Java or C++. Classes in ES6 provide a cleaner and more concise syntax for defining object blueprints and encapsulating behavior, making it easier to organize and maintain complex codebases.

Another important addition to ES6 is the Promise object, which provides a standardized mechanism for representing asynchronous operations and managing asynchronous code flows. Promises simplify the process of working with asynchronous code, replacing complex nested callback patterns with a more readable and composable syntax. Promises are widely used in modern

JavaScript development for handling asynchronous tasks such as fetching data from APIs, performing I/O operations, and managing asynchronous events.

Furthermore, ES6 introduced the async/await syntax, which builds on top of Promises to provide a more intuitive and synchronous-looking syntax for working with asynchronous code. Async/await allows developers to write asynchronous code in a synchronous style, making it simpler to reason about and debug asynchronous code flows. Async/await syntax is widely used in modern JavaScript development for its readability, simplicity, and compatibility with existing Promise-based APIs.

ES6 also introduced a range of other features and enhancements, including default function parameters, rest parameters, enhanced object literals, Map and Set data structures, symbols, iterators, and generators. These features have since become integral parts of modern JavaScript development, enabling developers to write cleaner, more expressive, and more maintainable code.

In conclusion, ECMAScript 6 (ES6) introduced a wide range of new features, syntax enhancements, and improvements to the JavaScript language, revolutionizing the way developers write and maintain JavaScript code. From block-scoped variables and arrow functions to template literals, spread operators, and async/await syntax, ES6 has significantly improved the readability, expressiveness, and functionality of JavaScript, making it a more powerful and versatile language for building modern web applications. As developers continue to embrace ES6 and its features, the JavaScript ecosystem will continue to evolve, innovate, and push the boundaries of what is possible with the language.

Arrow functions

Arrow functions, a feature introduced in ECMAScript 6 (ES6), have significantly transformed the way JavaScript developers write and structure their code. These functions offer a concise and expressive syntax for defining functions, providing several advantages over traditional function expressions. One of the primary benefits of arrow functions is their shorter syntax, which can drastically enhance code readability and reduce unnecessary boilerplate. Unlike traditional function expressions, arrow functions do not require the function keyword or curly braces for single-line expressions, making them ideal for writing compact and expressive code. This streamlined syntax allows developers to focus more on the logic of their functions rather than worrying about syntax overhead.

Another key advantage of arrow functions is their lexical scoping of the this keyword. In traditional JavaScript functions, the value of this is dynamically scoped based on how the function is called, often leading to confusion and unexpected behavior. However, arrow functions lexically bind the value of this to the surrounding lexical context, ensuring that the value of this remains consistent and predictable regardless of how the function is invoked. This behavior makes arrow functions particularly useful in callback functions and event handlers, where maintaining the correct context of this is crucial for proper functionality.

Additionally, arrow functions offer implicit return statements for single-line expressions, further reducing the verbosity of code and enhancing readability. When the body of an arrow function consists of a single expression, the return keyword is automatically implied, allowing developers to write more concise and expressive code without sacrificing clarity. This feature can significantly streamline code and make it easier to understand at a glance, especially for functions with straightforward logic or transformations.

However, it's essential to note that arrow functions have some limitations compared to traditional functions. For example, arrow functions do not have their own arguments object, which contains the arguments passed to the function. Instead, arrow functions inherit the arguments object from the surrounding lexical scope. Consequently, arrow functions cannot be used as constructors and cannot be called with the new keyword since they lack their own arguments or prototype objects. Moreover, arrow functions cannot be used as methods within objects since they do not have their own this value and inherit the this value from the surrounding lexical context.

Despite these limitations, arrow functions have become a fundamental part of modern JavaScript development, thanks to their concise syntax, lexical scoping behavior, and implicit return statements. They are widely utilized in functional programming paradigms, asynchronous code, and modern JavaScript frameworks such as React and Vue.js. When employed appropriately, arrow functions can significantly enhance code readability, reduce boilerplate, and make JavaScript code more expressive and maintainable.

In conclusion, arrow functions introduced in ECMAScript 6 (ES6) have revolutionized the way developers write JavaScript code, providing a more concise and expressive syntax for defining functions. With their shorter syntax, lexical scoping behavior, and implicit return statements, arrow functions have become an integral feature of modern JavaScript development, enabling developers to write cleaner, more readable, as well as more maintainable code. Despite their limitations, such as their handling of the this keyword and lack of arguments object, arrow functions remain a powerful and versatile tool in the JavaScript developer's toolkit, making it easier to write functional, expressive, and efficient code.

Template literals

Template literals, introduced in ECMAScript 6 (ES6), are a powerful feature that enhances the way developers work with strings in JavaScript. Unlike traditional strings, which are delimited by single or double quotes, template literals are enclosed in backticks (`), allowing for more expressive and flexible string formatting. Template literals support interpolation, multiline strings, and embedded expressions, providing developers with a more concise and readable syntax for working with strings.

One of the key aspects of template literals is string interpolation, which allows variables and expressions to be embedded directly within the string. This is achieved by enclosing the variable or expression in curly braces (${...}), which are then replaced with the corresponding value when the template literal is evaluated. String interpolation eliminates the need for concatenation or complex string manipulation, making code more readable and maintainable. Additionally, interpolation supports any valid JavaScript expression, allowing developers to embed dynamic content, perform calculations, or call functions within template literals.

Another significant advantage of template literals is their support for multiline strings. Traditionally, multiline strings in JavaScript required concatenating multiple strings with newline characters (\n), which could lead to verbose and hard-to-read code. Template literals, on the other hand, allow developers to create multiline strings simply by including line breaks within the backticks. This makes it easier to write and format multiline strings, particularly for tasks such as formatting HTML, generating SQL queries, or writing documentation.

Template literals also support embedded expressions, which allow for more complex string manipulation and formatting. Embedded expressions can include not only variables and simple expressions but also function calls, ternary operators, and even other template literals. This flexibility enables developers to create highly dynamic and expressive strings, allowing for more sophisticated string formatting and manipulation.

Furthermore, template literals support tagged templates, a feature that permits developers to customize the behavior of template literals by prefixing them with a function. Tagged templates receive the template literal as an array of strings (representing the static parts of the template) and the interpolated values as separate arguments. This enables advanced string manipulation and localization, allowing developers to implement custom formatting, localization, or security features directly within the template literal syntax.

Despite their many advantages, it's essential to consider potential drawbacks when using template literals. Template literals are not supported in older browsers that do not support ES6, so developers may need to transpile code using tools like Babel to ensure compatibility. Additionally, excessive use of template literals with complex expressions or logic embedded within them can lead to code that is challenging to read and maintain. It's important to strike a balance between the convenience and readability offered by template literals and the maintainability of the codebase.

In conclusion, template literals are a powerful and versatile feature introduced in ECMAScript 6 (ES6) that significantly enhance the way developers work with strings in JavaScript. Their support for string interpolation, multiline strings, and embedded expressions provides developers with a more expressive and readable syntax for string formatting and manipulation. While template literals offer numerous benefits, it's essential to use them judiciously and consider potential compatibility and maintainability concerns. Overall, template literals have become an essential tool in the JavaScript developer's toolkit, enabling more efficient and expressive string handling in modern web development.

Destructuring assignments

Destructuring assignment, introduced in ECMAScript 6 (ES6), is a powerful feature that provides a concise and expressive syntax for extracting values from arrays or objects and assigning them to variables. This feature simplifies the process of working with complex data structures, reducing the need for manual extraction and enabling more declarative and readable code. Destructuring assignment allows developers to unpack values from arrays or objects into distinct variables using a syntax that mirrors the structure of the data being deconstructed.

One of the primary use cases for destructuring assignment is extracting values from arrays. With destructuring assignment, developers can specify variable names enclosed in square brackets ([...]) on the left side of the assignment operator (=) to capture values from corresponding positions in the array. This allows for easy extraction of individual elements or subsets of elements from arrays without needing to access them directly by index. Additionally, destructuring assignment supports skipping elements or capturing remaining elements into a single variable using the rest (...) syntax, providing flexibility and convenience when working with arrays of varying lengths.

Similarly, destructuring assignment can be used to extract values from objects by specifying variable names enclosed in curly braces ({...}) on the left side of the assignment operator. The variable names correspond to the keys of the object, allowing developers to access object properties directly without needing to reference them by name. This makes code more self-descriptive and less error-prone, as developers can clearly see which properties are being extracted from the object.

Destructuring assignment also supports nested structures, allowing developers to destructure values from nested arrays or objects in a single expression. This enables more complex data manipulation and extraction, such as extracting values from nested arrays or accessing deeply nested object properties with ease. By providing a concise and expressive syntax for working with nested data structures, destructuring assignment simplifies code and improves readability, particularly in scenarios where data manipulation is frequent or complex.

Furthermore, destructuring assignment can be used in function parameter lists to destructure values directly from function arguments. This enables developers to access specific properties or elements of complex objects or arrays passed as arguments to functions without needing to manually extract them within the function body. This makes function signatures more descriptive and self-contained, improving code clarity and reducing the need for additional parameter handling logic within function implementations.

Despite its many advantages, it's essential to consider potential drawbacks when using destructuring assignment. While destructuring assignment can make code more concise and expressive, excessive use of nested destructuring or complex destructuring expressions can lead to code that is difficult to understand and maintain. It's important to strike a balance between the convenience and readability offered by destructuring assignment and the maintainability of the codebase.

In conclusion, destructuring assignment is a powerful feature introduced in ECMAScript 6 (ES6) that simplifies the process of working with complex data structures in JavaScript. Its concise and expressive syntax allows developers to extract values from arrays or objects with ease, improving code readability and minimithe need for manual extraction and manipulation. By providing a more declarative and self-descriptive way to work with data, destructuring assignment enhances code clarity and maintainability, making it an essential tool in the JavaScript developer's toolkit.

Spread and rest operators

The spread and rest operators, introduced in ECMAScript 6 (ES6), are powerful features that enhance the way JavaScript developers work with arrays and function parameters. These operators provide concise and expressive syntax for manipulating arrays and handling function arguments, offering greater flexibility and convenience in modern JavaScript development. The spread operator (...) allows developers to expand an iterable (such as an array) into individual elements, while the rest operator (...) enables the collection of multiple elements into a single array. Together, these operators streamline common tasks such as array concatenation, copying, and function parameter handling, making code more readable and maintainable.

The spread operator (...) is primarily used to expand an iterable into individual elements, allowing for easy manipulation and composition of arrays. When used in array literals or function calls, the spread operator spreads the elements of an array or other iterable, such as a string or a Set, into individual elements. This enables tasks such as concatenating arrays, copying arrays, or passing multiple arguments to functions without needing to manually construct or manipulate arrays. The spread operator also allows for the creation of shallow copies of arrays, ensuring that changes to the copied array don't affect the original array. Additionally, the spread operator can be used to merge objects by spreading their properties into a new object, providing a concise and efficient way to combine object properties.

On the other hand, the rest operator (...) is used to collect multiple elements into a single array, providing a convenient way to handle variable numbers of function arguments. When used in function parameter lists, the rest operator collects any remaining arguments into an array, allowing functions to accept a variable number of arguments without needing to specify them individually. This makes functions more flexible and adaptable to different use cases, enabling developers to create functions that can accept any number of arguments and operate on them dynamically. The rest operator also simplifies function parameter handling by providing a concise and expressive syntax for working with variable-length argument lists.

One common use case for the spread and rest operators is in array manipulation, where they provide a more expressive and concise syntax for common array operations. For example, the spread operator can be used to concatenate arrays, merge arrays, or clone arrays, while the rest operator can be used to extract or collect multiple elements into a single array. These operators streamline array manipulation tasks, reducing the need for manual iteration or construction of arrays and improving code readability and maintainability.

In addition to array manipulation, the spread and rest operators are widely used in function parameter handling, where they enable functions to accept and work with variable numbers of arguments. By using the rest operator in function parameter lists, developers can create functions that accept any number of arguments, providing greater flexibility and adaptability. This is particularly useful in scenarios where functions need to operate on variable-length argument lists or where the number of arguments may vary dynamically at runtime.

Despite their many advantages, it's essential to consider potential drawbacks when using the spread and rest operators. While these operators provide a concise and expressive syntax for array manipulation and function parameter handling, excessive use of nested spread or rest operations can lead to code that is challenging to read and understand. It's important to strike a balance between the convenience and readability offered by these operators and the maintainability of the codebase.

In conclusion, the spread and rest operators are powerful features introduced in ECMAScript 6 (ES6) that enhance the way JavaScript developers work with arrays and function parameters. These operators provide concise and expressive syntax for array manipulation and function parameter handling, streamlining common tasks and improving code readability and maintainability. By leveraging the spread and rest operators, developers can write more expressive and flexible code, enabling them to create more efficient and adaptable JavaScript applications.

CHAPTER VII

Introduction to Frameworks and Libraries

Overview of popular JavaScript frameworks and libraries (e.g., React, Angular, Vue.js)

JavaScript frameworks and libraries have become essential tools in modern web development, empowering developers to create dynamic and interactive user interfaces with ease. Among the myriad of options available, three stand out as the most popular and widely adopted: React, Angular, and Vue.js. These frameworks have garnered significant attention and adoption within the developer community, each offering unique features, strengths, and use cases.

React, developed by Facebook, is a declarative, component-based library for building user interfaces. Its core philosophy revolves around the concept of reusable components, which encapsulate UI logic and behavior into modular units. This approach facilitates the creation of complex UIs by composing components together, making it easier to manage and maintain large-scale applications. React's virtual DOM efficiently updates and re-renders components when underlying data changes, resulting in improved performance and user experience. Its popularity is further boosted by a vibrant ecosystem and strong community support, with a plethora of third-party libraries, tools, as well as resources available to streamline development.

Angular, developed by Google, takes a more comprehensive and opinionated approach to front-end development. It provides a full-fledged solution for building web applications, offering features including two- way data binding, dependency injection, routing, as well as state management out of the box. Angular's architecture follows the Model-View-Controller (MVC) pattern, with components acting as the foundations of the application. Despite its steep learning curve and sometimes verbose syntax, Angular remains a preferred choice for enterprise-scale applications due to its robustness, scalability, and comprehensive feature set. Its built-in tooling and testing capabilities, along with the Angular CLI, simplify project setup and maintenance, ensuring reliability and efficiency.

On the other hand, Vue.js, created by Evan You, stands out for its simplicity, flexibility, and ease of integration. It is a progressive framework that is equally suited for small-scale projects and large-scale applications. Vue.js's reactive data binding system and virtual DOM implementation ensure efficient updates and optimal performance, while its component-based architecture promotes reusability and maintainability. Its gentle learning curve and approachable syntax make it accessible to developers of every skill levels, attracting a diverse and inclusive community of users. Additionally, Vue.js's ecosystem is rapidly expanding, with an abundance of plugins, extensions, and community-driven resources available to enhance development productivity.

While React, Angular, and Vue.js are the frontrunners in front-end development, it's important to acknowledge that each framework has its own strengths and weaknesses, and the choice of framework ultimately depends on the specific requirements and preferences of the project. React excels in building reusable and performant UI components, Angular offers a comprehensive solution for large-scale applications with built-in features, and Vue.js provides a lightweight and flexible framework with a gentle learning curve. Regardless of the choice, developers can leverage these frameworks and libraries to create powerful, responsive, and engaging user experiences on the web.

As the landscape of web development evolves, React, Angular, and Vue.js are expected to maintain their prominence, driving innovation and pushing the boundaries of front-end development. Their active communities, robust ecosystems, and ongoing development ensure that developers have access to the tools as well as resources they need to build modern web applications effectively. Whether it's creating a simple website or a complex web application, these frameworks and libraries enable developers to bring their ideas to life and deliver exceptional user experiences on the web.

Understanding the role of frameworks in web development

Frameworks serve as foundational pillars in the realm of web development, reshaping the manner in which developers craft and deploy applications across the internet. These tools encompass pre-written code, libraries, and utilities designed to provide a structured base for developing web applications. By offering standardized patterns, conventions, and resources, frameworks streamline development processes and address common challenges inherent in web application development.

A fundamental role of frameworks in web development is the provision of structure and organization to codebases. Through enforcement of architectural patterns like Model-View-Controller (MVC) or Model-View-ViewModel (MVVM), frameworks assist developers in organizing code into manageable components, thereby separating concerns and fostering maintainability. This structured approach facilitates comprehensibility, upkeep, and scalability of applications over time, resulting in more resilient and sustainable codebases.

Moreover, frameworks facilitate code reuse and modularity, allowing developers to harness existing components and libraries to construct new applications more efficiently. Many frameworks come equipped with built-in features and functionalities such as routing, form validation, and data fetching, which can be seamlessly integrated into applications without necessitating extensive custom development. This modular approach promotes code reuse, minimizes redundancy, and expedites development cycles, empowering developers to concentrate on creating unique and innovative features rather than reinventing the wheel.

Additionally, frameworks play a vital role in standardizing development practices and fostering best practices within the developer community. By establishing conventions and guidelines for code organization, naming conventions, and project structure, frameworks promote coherence and consistency across projects. This standardization fosters collaboration, code sharing, and facilitates the onboarding process for new team members, cultivating a more unified and productive development environment.

Another significant role of frameworks in web development is to abstract away low-level implementation details, providing higher-level abstractions that simplify complex tasks. For instance, frameworks often address browser compatibility issues, performance optimizations, and security concerns behind the scenes, enabling developers to focus on building features instead of grappling with platform-specific intricacies. This abstraction layer shields developers from the intricacies of web development, empowering them to be more efficient and creative in their endeavors.

Frameworks also serve as catalysts for innovation, driving progress and pushing the boundaries of web development. By furnishing developers with potent tools, libraries, and patterns, frameworks encourage experimentation, rapid prototyping, and iteration on solutions. Frameworks such as React, Angular, and Vue.js have catalyzed a wave of innovation in front-end development, giving rise to novel paradigms like component-based architecture, reactive programming, and server-side rendering.

Furthermore, frameworks foster vibrant ecosystems and communities that provide developers with a wealth of resources, including documentation, tutorials, forums, and third-party plugins. These communities cultivate collaboration, knowledge sharing, and continuous learning, enabling developers to stay abreast of the latest trends and technologies in web development. Additionally, frameworks boast extensive libraries of third-party plugins and extensions that extend their functionality and enrich applications, further expediting development workflows and broadening the capabilities of applications.

In conclusion, frameworks serve as multifaceted enablers in web development, furnishing structure, organization, abstraction, and innovation to the development process. By standardizing development practices, promoting code reuse, abstracting away complexity, and fostering collaboration and innovation, frameworks empower developers to construct potent, scalable, and maintainable web applications more efficiently. As the landscape of web development evolves, frameworks will remain indispensable tools for developers, equipping them to tackle increasingly complex challenges and deliver exceptional user experiences on the web.

Choosing the right framework for your project

Choosing the proper framework for a project is considered as a critical decision that can significantly impact its success and long-term viability. With a plethora of frameworks available in the web development ecosystem, ranging from full-fledged platforms like Angular and React to lightweight libraries like Vue.js and Svelte, developers must carefully evaluate various factors to determine which framework best aligns with their project's requirements, goals, and constraints.

One of the primary considerations when choosing a framework is the specific needs and goals of the project. Different frameworks are optimized for different use cases, whether it's building single-page applications (SPAs), progressive web apps (PWAs), or large-scale enterprise applications. By identifying the project's requirements and objectives upfront, developers can narrow down their options and focus on frameworks that are best suited to meet those needs.

Another important factor to consider is the project's technical requirements and constraints. This includes factors such as performance considerations, scalability requirements, browser compatibility, and integration with existing systems or technologies. For example, if the project requires high performance and real-time updates, a framework like React with its virtual DOM may be a better fit. On the other hand, if the project prioritizes simplicity and ease of adoption, a lightweight framework like Vue.js or Svelte may be more appropriate.

Additionally, developers should consider their team's expertise and familiarity with the framework ecosystem. Choosing a framework that are in line with the team's skills and experience can streamline development workflows, reduce ramp-up time, and minimize the risk of technical debt. It's essential to assess the availability of resources, documentation, and community support for the chosen framework, as these factors can significantly impact the project's success and maintainability in the long run.

Furthermore, developers should evaluate the framework's ecosystem and ecosystem compatibility. A robust ecosystem with a thriving community of developers, third-party libraries, tools, and plugins can enhance productivity and provide solutions to common challenges. It's important to assess factors such as library availability, community activity, and ecosystem maturity when choosing a framework, as these factors can influence the project's ability to scale and evolve over time.

Cost considerations are also important when selecting a framework for a project. While many frameworks are open-source and free to use, there may be associated costs such as training, support, or licensing fees for certain features or tools. It's necessary to evaluate the total cost of ownership (TCO) of each framework, including both direct and indirect costs, to ensure that it aligns with the project's budget and resource constraints.

Finally, developers should consider the long-term implications of their framework choice, including factors such as vendor lock-in, maintenance overhead, and future-proofing. While it's impossible to predict the future, choosing a framework with a strong track record of stability, backward compatibility, and community support can mitigate the risk of obsolescence and ensure the project's longevity.

In conclusion, choosing the right framework for a project needs careful consideration of different factors, including the project's requirements, technical constraints, team expertise, ecosystem compatibility, cost considerations, and long-term implications. By evaluating these factors thoughtfully and conducting thorough research and analysis, developers can make knowledgeable decisions that maximize the project's chances of success and ensure its long-term viability in an ever-evolving web development landscape.

CHAPTER VIII

Building Interactive Web Experiences

Introduction to building interactive web applications with JavaScript

Building interactive web applications with JavaScript is an exciting and rewarding endeavor that allows developers to create dynamic and engaging user experiences. JavaScript, as the main language of the web, plays a central role in enabling interactivity and responsiveness in modern web applications. Whether it's implementing client-side form validation, creating interactive charts and graphs, or building real-time chat applications, JavaScript provides the tools and capabilities needed to bring web applications to life.

At its core, building interactive web applications with JavaScript involves manipulating the Document Object Model (DOM), which represents the structure of a web page as a hierarchical tree of objects. By using JavaScript to access and manipulate DOM elements, developers can dynamically update the content, styling, and behavior of web pages in response to user interactions or other events. This allows for the creation of interactive features such as dropdown menus, sliders, and accordions, enhancing the user experience and making web applications more engaging and intuitive to use.

One of the key principles of building interactive web applications with JavaScript is event-driven programming. In event-driven programming, interactions or actions by the user, such as clicking a button or submitting a form, trigger events that can be captured and handled by JavaScript code. By listening for and responding to these events, developers can establish interactive and responsive user interfaces that react dynamically to user input. Event-driven programming enables a wide range of interactive features, from simple animations and transitions to complex workflows and workflows.

Another important concept in building interactive web applications is asynchronous programming. Asynchronous programming allows JavaScript code to execute non-blocking operations, such as fetching data from a server or performing calculations, without halting the execution of other code. This is particularly important for building responsive and performant web applications, as it ensures that the user interface remains responsive even when performing time-consuming tasks in the background. Asynchronous programming is typically achieved using callbacks, promises, or async/await syntax, which allow developers to manage asynchronous operations and handle the results or errors asynchronously.

In addition to event-driven and asynchronous programming, building interactive web applications with JavaScript often involves working with external libraries and frameworks. Libraries like jQuery provide utilities and abstractions for common tasks such as DOM manipulation, event handling, and AJAX requests, simplifying development and reducing boilerplate code. Meanwhile, frameworks like React, Angular, and Vue.js offer more comprehensive solutions for building complex user interfaces, providing tools for component-based architecture, state management, and routing.

Furthermore, building interactive web applications with JavaScript often involves integrating with other web technologies and APIs, such as HTML5, CSS3, and various web APIs (e.g., Geolocation API, WebSockets API). These technologies enable developers to leverage native browser capabilities and access device features, enabling more immersive and feature-rich web applications. For example, HTML5 canvas and WebGL APIs allow for the creation of interactive graphics and animations, while the Web Audio API enables audio synthesis and processing in web applications.

In conclusion, building interactive web applications with JavaScript is a multifaceted and dynamic process that involves manipulating the DOM, handling events, and executing asynchronous operations. By leveraging event-driven programming, asynchronous programming, and external libraries and frameworks, developers can create rich and engaging user experiences that respond dynamically to user input and interactions. As the web continues to evolve and new technologies emerge, JavaScript remains at the forefront of web development, powering the next generation of interactive and immersive web applications.

Creating interactive forms

Creating interactive forms is a fundamental aspect of web development that allows developers to build user-friendly and engaging interfaces for collecting user input. Forms serve as the primary means for users to interact with web applications, enabling them to submit data, make selections, and perform various actions. JavaScript is crucial in enhancing the interactivity of forms by enabling dynamic validation, real-time feedback, and interactive features such as autocomplete and conditional logic. By leveraging JavaScript, developers can create forms that are more intuitive, responsive, and user-friendly, enhancing the overall user experience.

One of the key aspects of developing interactive forms with JavaScript is form validation. JavaScript can be employed to validate form input in real-time, providing instant feedback to users and preventing them from submitting invalid data. This can include checking for required fields, validating email addresses, enforcing minimum and maximum length constraints, and verifying the format of data such as dates and phone numbers. By validating form input on the client side, JavaScript reduces the likelihood of errors and invalid submissions, improving data quality and user satisfaction.

Additionally, JavaScript enables developers to enhance the user experience of forms by adding interactive features such as autocomplete and suggestions. Autocomplete functionality can be implemented using JavaScript to provide users with suggestions or predictions based on their input, helping them quickly and accurately complete form fields. This is particularly useful for fields like addresses, names, and product searches, where users may benefit from suggestions to streamline the input process and reduce errors.

Conditional logic is another powerful feature enabled by JavaScript that can be used to create dynamic and interactive forms. With conditional logic, developers can show or hide form fields, sections, or entire form elements based on the user's input or selections. This allows for more personalized and context-aware forms, where the user experience adapts dynamically based on the user's actions. For example, a form might display additional fields or options based on the user's selection of a certain checkbox or dropdown menu, providing a more tailored and streamlined experience.

Furthermore, JavaScript can be used to implement features such as form submission handling and error messaging. By intercepting form submissions and handling them programmatically, developers can perform additional validation, data processing, or server-side interactions before submitting the form data to the server.

JavaScript can also be used to display error messages or notifications to users when validation errors occur, helping them identify and correct mistakes more easily.

Another important aspect of creating interactive forms with JavaScript is accessibility. It's crucial to ensure that forms are accessible to users with disabilities and/or impairments, such as screen readers or keyboard-only navigation. JavaScript can be used to enhance the accessibility of forms by ensuring that they are properly labeled, structured, and navigable using keyboard shortcuts or assistive technologies. This includes providing descriptive labels, using ARIA (Accessible Rich Internet Applications) attributes, and ensuring that form elements are focusable and operable with keyboard input.

In conclusion, creating interactive forms with JavaScript is essential for building user-friendly and engaging web applications. JavaScript enables developers to add dynamic validation, real-time feedback, interactive features, and accessibility enhancements to forms, improving the overall user experience and usability. By leveraging JavaScript effectively, developers can create forms that are intuitive, responsive, as well as accessible to all users, enhancing the success and effectiveness of their web applications.

Implementing animations and transitions

Implementing animations and transitions is a powerful technique in web development that can greatly improve the user experience and visual appeal of a website or web application. Animations and transitions allow developers to add dynamic movement, visual effects, and interactive elements to web pages, making them more engaging and intuitive to use. With the advent of modern web technologies such as CSS3 and JavaScript, implementing animations and transitions has become more accessible and flexible than ever before.

CSS3 provides a rich set of features for creating animations and transitions directly within stylesheets, without the need for complex JavaScript code. CSS animations allow developers to define keyframes and specify how properties change over time, enabling the creation of complex animations such as fades, slides, rotations, and scale transformations. CSS transitions, on the other hand, enable smooth transitions between different states or styles of an element, including changing its color, size, or position in response to user interactions or other events. By leveraging CSS animations and transitions, developers can create visually stunning effects that enhance the overall user experience without relying on external libraries or plugins.

In addition to CSS, JavaScript can be used to implement more advanced and interactive animations on the web. JavaScript libraries such as GreenSock (GSAP) and Anime.js provide powerful tools for creating complex animations with precise control over timing, easing, and sequencing. These libraries enable developers to create animations that respond to user input, synchronize with other elements on the page, or dynamically update based on changes in data or state. JavaScript animations are particularly useful for creating interactive effects such as parallax scrolling, draggable elements, and interactive charts or graphs.

One of the key considerations when implementing animations and transitions is performance. While animations and transitions can enhance the user experience, poorly optimized animations can lead to performance issues such as stuttering, jank, or excessive battery drain on mobile devices. To ensure smooth and responsive animations, developers should strive to minimize the use of expensive CSS properties such as transform and opacity, use hardware-accelerated animations whenever possible, and optimize animations for performance by reducing the number of elements being animated and avoiding complex animations that require frequent repaints or reflows.

Another important consideration is accessibility. Animations and transitions should be designed with accessibility in mind, ensuring that they are usable and understandable for all users, including those with disabilities or impairments. This includes providing alternative means of interaction or feedback for users who may have difficulty perceiving or interacting with animated elements, such as providing visual cues, keyboard shortcuts, or accessible controls. Developers should also ensure that animations do not interfere with screen readers or other assistive technologies used by users with disabilities.

Furthermore, animations and transitions should be used judiciously and purposefully to enhance the user experience, rather than simply for the sake of adding visual flair. Overuse of animations can be distracting or overwhelming for users, detracting from the usability and effectiveness of the website or web application. Developers should carefully consider the context and purpose of each animation, focusing on enhancing clarity, usability, and engagement without overshadowing or detracting from the content or functionality of the site.

In conclusion, implementing animations and transitions is a powerful technique for enhancing the user experience and visual appeal of web applications. By leveraging CSS, JavaScript, and modern web technologies, developers can create dynamic and engaging animations that captivate users and improve usability. However, it's essential to consider factors such as performance, accessibility, and purpose when implementing animations, ensuring that they enhance rather than detract from the overall user experience. With careful planning and execution, animations and transitions can elevate the quality and effectiveness of web applications, making them more memorable, enjoyable, and impactful for users.

Integrating third-party APIs

Integrating third-party APIs is a common practice in modern web development, enabling developers to leverage the functionality and data provided by external services to enhance the features and capabilities of their applications. Third-party APIs, or Application Programming Interfaces, expose specific endpoints and methods that developers can interact with programmatically to access resources, perform actions, or retrieve data. These APIs cover a wide range of services and functionalities, including social media platforms, payment gateways, mapping services, weather forecasts, and more. By integrating third-party APIs into their applications, developers can save time and also effort by leveraging existing solutions and focusing on core application logic rather than reinventing the wheel.

One of the main advantages of integrating third-party APIs is the ability to access external data and services that would otherwise be challenging or time-consuming to implement from scratch. For example, integrating the Google Maps API allows developers to embed interactive maps into their applications and provide features such as geolocation, routing, and place search without having to build these functionalities themselves. Similarly, integrating social media APIs enables developers to incorporate social sharing, authentication, and user profile integration seamlessly into their applications, enhancing user engagement and connectivity.

Another benefit of integrating third-party APIs is the opportunity to extend the functionality of an application by leveraging specialized services and tools provided by external providers. For example, integrating payment gateway APIs such as Stripe or PayPal allows developers to accept payments securely and efficiently, enabling e-commerce functionality in their applications. Likewise, integrating communication APIs such as Twilio or SendGrid enables developers to add features such as SMS messaging, email notifications, and voice calling to their applications, enhancing communication and engagement with users.

Furthermore, integrating third-party APIs can improve the scalability and performance of an application by offloading resource-intensive tasks or delegating specialized functionalities to external services. For example, integrating cloud storage APIs such as Amazon S3 or Google Cloud Storage allows developers to store and retrieve large amounts of data efficiently, reducing the burden on their own servers and improving scalability. Similarly, integrating content delivery network (CDN) APIs such as Cloudflare or Akamai enables developers to deliver static assets and content to users more quickly and reliably, improving performance and user experience.

However, integrating third-party APIs also comes with challenges and considerations that developers must address to ensure the reliability, security, and maintainability of their applications. For example, developers must carefully review and understand the documentation and terms of service of each API to ensure compliance with usage limits, pricing plans, and data usage policies. Additionally, developers must handle errors and exceptions gracefully, implement proper error handling and fallback mechanisms, and monitor API usage and performance to detect and address issues proactively.

Security is another critical consideration when integrating third-party APIs, as it involves transmitting sensitive data and interacting with external services that may pose security risks. Developers must implement secure authentication and authorization mechanisms, such as

OAuth or API keys, to guarantee that only authorized users as well as applications can access the API. Additionally, developers must validate and sanitize input data, encrypt sensitive information, and implement measures such as rate limiting and throttling to prevent abuse and mitigate security threats.

In conclusion, integrating third-party APIs is a valuable practice in modern web development that enables developers to extend the functionality, access external services, and improve the scalability as well as performance of their applications. By leveraging the capabilities and resources provided by third-party APIs, developers can save time and effort, enhance the features and capabilities of their applications, and deliver more powerful and compelling user experiences. However, developers must also address challenges such as compliance, security, and reliability to ensure the successful integration and operation of third-party APIs in their applications. With careful planning, implementation, and monitoring, integrating third-party APIs can be a valuable asset in building robust, scalable, and feature-rich web applications.

CHAPTER IX

Optimizing JavaScript Performance

Techniques for improving JavaScript performance

Enhancing the performance of JavaScript is an essential component of web development since it has a direct influence on the user experience, the amount of time it takes for pages to load, and the general responsiveness of different web apps. Sluggish speed, higher resource consumption, and a poorer user experience can be the result of inefficient code and bad optimization practices when using JavaScript, despite the fact that JavaScript is a powerful and versatile programming language. Developers are fortunate in that they have access to a variety of methods and best practices that may be utilized to optimize JavaScript code and enhance performance.

The optimization of code execution and the reduction of superfluous overhead are two of the most efficient strategies for enhancing the performance of JavaScript. To accomplish this, it is necessary to identify and remove performance bottlenecks, which may include excessive manipulation of the document object model (DOM), inefficient loops, and unnecessary calculations. It is possible for developers to enhance the execution of code by reducing the number of costly actions, such as nested loops or recursive functions, and by optimizing algorithms for efficiency. In addition, in order to lessen the amount of overhead and enhance efficiency, developers should steer clear of creating objects, calling methods, and allocating memory than is absolutely necessary.

The reduction of network requests and the optimization of resource loading are two additional essential techniques that can be employed to enhance the performance of JavaScript. approaches such as bundling and minification are included in this category. These approaches minimize the size of JavaScript files by combining many files into a single bundle and removing whitespace, comments, and characters that are not essential. Caching static assets and reducing server load can be accomplished by developers through the utilization of browser caching and content delivery networks (CDNs). This results in improved load times and user responsiveness. In addition, developers should give priority to crucial resources and lazy-load assets that are not essential in order to guarantee that the most important material loads in a timely and effective manner.

In addition, one of the most important things that can be done to improve the perceived speed and responsiveness of online apps is to optimize the rendering performance. Specifically, this entails minimizing layout thrashing, which is a phenomenon that takes place when the browser continually recalculates the arrangement of components on the page. This can result in animations that are janky and stuttering. The performance of rendering can be improved by developers by decreasing the number of reflows and repaints, utilizing CSS transformations and animations to achieve smoother transitions, and optimizing CSS selectors and styles to reduce the amount of rendering overhead. Additionally, developers should avoid blocking the main thread with JavaScript processes that are running for an extended period of time. This might result in the page becoming sluggish, which has a poor impact on the user experience.

In close connection with rendering performance is the optimization of transitions and animations that are written in JavaScript. Web applications frequently make use of animations and transitions in order to improve their visual appeal and level of interactivity. However, animations that are not properly optimized can result in jank, stuttering, and a decrease in performance performance. It is possible for developers to enhance the performance of animations by utilizing hardware-accelerated CSS attributes, such as transform and opacity, to offload animations to the graphics processing unit (GPU) and generate motion that is smoother and more realistic. If developers want to schedule animations and transitions, they should use the requestAnimationFrame() function. This will ensure that the animations and transitions run at a steady frame rate and reduce jank and stuttering throughout the animation.

For the purpose of finding and diagnosing performance issues in JavaScript code, it is vital to make use of browser performance tools and techniques for profiling. Chrome DevTools and Firefox Developer Tools are examples of browser developer tools that offer powerful profiling and debugging features. These tools enable developers to monitor the use of the central processing unit (CPU), the consumption of memory, the activity on the network, and the rendering performance. These tools allow developers to detect areas for optimization and execute specific enhancements in order to increase the overall performance of JavaScript. They do this by identifying performance bottlenecks and hotspots to improve overall performance.

In conclusion, enhancing the performance of JavaScript is essential in order to offer online applications that are quick, responsive, and efficient. JavaScript code can be optimized and the user experience can be improved by developers through the utilization of several strategies. These techniques include optimizing code execution, limiting network requests, optimizing rendering performance, and leveraging browser performance capabilities. By making performance optimization a top priority and putting best practices into action, developers can ensure that their web apps load quickly, respond without any hiccups, and provide a seamless user experience across an array of browsers and devices.

Minification and bundling

Minification and bundling are two strategies that are vital in modern web development when it comes to optimizing the performance and efficiency of JavaScript code. Both of these techniques play a crucial role in the process. The term "minification" refers to the process of lowering the size of JavaScript files by deleting characters that are not required, such as whitespace, comments, and redundant code. This leads to smaller file sizes, which in turn leads to faster download times and reduced network latency when loading web pages. Consequently, this results in a number of benefits. The general performance and responsiveness of web applications can be improved by developers through the process of minifying JavaScript code. This is especially beneficial for users who are connected to networks that are slow or have limited bandwidth.

The process of bundling, on the other hand, includes integrating a number of JavaScript files into a single bundle or package. This helps reduce the amount of HTTP requests that are necessary to retrieve JavaScript resources, which increases the likelihood that page load speeds will be greatly improved, particularly on networks that have a high latency. As a result of the fact that browsers are able to cache a single packaged file more effectively than several individual files, bundling also makes it easier to compress and cache JavaScript files. Additionally, developers are able to more effectively organize and manage their code through the use of bundling, which simplifies the process of development and deployment.

In conjunction with one another, minification and bundling constitute a powerful optimization technique for

JavaScript code. This strategy enables developers to provide web apps that are smaller, load more quickly, and offer a more satisfying experience to users. It is possible for developers to minimize the overall file size of their online apps by minifying and bundling JavaScript code. As a result, load times are reduced, and performance is improved across a wide variety of devices as well as network conditions. Additionally, minification and bundling help to improve the development process by minimizing the number of files that need to be handled and distributed. This results in workflows that are more efficient and iteration cycles that are completed more quickly.

Minification and bundling are two optimization techniques that are frequently used in conjunction with other optimization strategies, such as tree shaking and code splitting, in order to further enhance the effectiveness and performance of JavaScript code. Tree shaking, for instance, is the process of deleting unneeded or dead code from JavaScript bundles. This helps to reduce the size of the bundles even more and eliminates any unnecessary overhead. Rather than providing all of the JavaScript code in a single bundle, code splitting enables developers to dynamically load JavaScript code on demand. This has the potential to significantly reduce the amount of time that it requires for a page to load initially, and it may also boost the speed of the entire process.

Although minification and bundling offer considerable performance gains, developers must also be aware of potential pitfalls and considerations when applying these approaches. Minification and bundling are two related techniques. By way of illustration, minification can occasionally result in unforeseen side effects or problems if it is not carried out with caution. This is because the removal of particular characters or code can potentially change the behavior of the JavaScript framework. Similar to the previous point, bundling can result in increased complexity and overhead, particularly for bigger web applications that have a high number of dependencies or requirements for dynamic code splitting. The developers have to find a way to optimize the size of the code while also keeping readability, maintainability, and compatibility with other tools and libraries when they are working on the project.

When it comes to increasing the performance and efficiency of JavaScript code in modern web development, minification and bundling are two strategies that are absolutely necessary. The use of minification and bundling enables developers to offer web applications that are faster, more responsive, and give a better user experience. This is accomplished by lowering the size of the files and minimizing the number of network calls. Developers are need to take into account potential downsides and trade-offs, as well as carefully balance optimization with other concerns such as readability, maintainability, and compatibility. Although these techniques offer significant performance improvements, developers must also factor in potential drawbacks and trade-offs. Minification and bundling are two techniques that, when used in conjunction with careful planning and implementation, can assist developers in the creation of web applications that are more portable, quicker, and more effective in meeting the requirements of modern users and devices.

Caching strategies

Instead of re-fetching or re-generating material from the original source, caching strategies are crucial components of web development that assist enhance the performance, scalability, and efficiency of online applications. This is accomplished by storing and providing content that has been previously fetched or generated from a cache. Caching is the process of keeping copies of data that is frequently accessed, such as web pages, photos, or API replies, in a temporary storage area, such as the cache of the browser or a cache on the server side, in order to increase efficiency and decrease the amount of bandwidth that is consumed. Developers are able to optimize the delivery of content, minimize the burden on servers, and improve the overall user experience when they make good use of caching solutions.

Browser caching is one of the most frequent caching tactics used in web development. This strategy involves saving static assets in the cache of the browser, such as HTML, CSS, JavaScript, and pictures. These assets are downloaded and cached locally by the browser whenever a user visits a website. This makes it possible for subsequent visits to the website to load more quickly since the assets can be accessed from the cache rather than being re-downloaded from the server and retrieved from the cache. Developers have the ability to manage the behavior of browser caching by providing suitable cache headers, such as Cache-manage and Expires, to determine the length of time that assets should be cached and the time at which they should delete themselves.

One further method of caching is known as server-side caching, which involves keeping content that is created or dynamic in a cache that is located on the server. This is done in order to reduce the amount of computational overhead that is required to generate the content for each request. The usage of server-side caching is especially beneficial for content that is either expensive or time-consuming to develop. Some examples of this type of content include database queries, API answers, and HTML pages that are generated dynamically. It is possible for servers to deliver successive requests for the same content more quickly and effectively if they cache the results of these operations in memory or on disk. This helps to reduce response times and the amount of strain that is placed on the server.

Additionally, content delivery networks (CDNs) offer caching solutions that help improve the performance and availability of web material by distributing it throughout a network of servers that are placed closer to end users. This helps enhance the overall performance of the web. Users are able to access material from servers that are physically closer to them, which reduces latency and improves load times. material delivery networks (CDNs) cache static assets such as photos, videos, and scripts on edge servers that are situated in various geographic regions. The content delivery networks (CDNs) offer a multitude of additional advantages, including load balancing, DDoS protection, and content optimization. These advantages make them an effective instrument for enhancing the performance and dependability of web services.

In addition, cache invalidation strategies can be used with caching strategies in order to guarantee that the content that is cached is always current and fresh. Cache invalidation is the proedure of removing or updating cached content when it gets stale or out of date. This can happen either because of a predetermined expiration time or because of changes in the data or resources that are being cached. Cache busting, versioning, and cache invalidation headers are some of the strategies that developers can use to govern when cached content should be refreshed or re-fetched. This ensures that consumers are always provided with the most recent and correct information possible.

When it comes to implementing caching in web applications, developers need to take into consideration potential downsides and trade-offs, despite the fact that caching solutions offer significant speed gains. Examples of problems that might arise as a result of caching include cache staleness, which occurs when users are offered content that is either out of date or has expired, resulting in information that is either inconsistent or wrong. The use of caching can also drain server resources and memory, particularly when the content being cached is substantial or often accessed. This can result in increased server expenses or a decrease of speed.

In conclusion, caching strategies are crucial components of web development that assist enhance the performance, scalability, and efficiency of web applications. They do this by storing and serving content that is frequently retrieved from a cache. The delivery of material may be optimized, server load can be reduced, and the overall user experience can be improved if developers make efficient use of cache invalidation techniques, server-side caching, content delivery networks (CDNs), and browser caching. While caching does give considerable performance benefits, developers must also take into account potential negatives and trade-offs. Additionally, they must carefully balance caching with other issues such as cache invalidation, cache freshness, and resource usage. Using caching solutions, developers may construct web applications that are faster, more efficient, and more scalable, all of which are designed to match the requirements of today's users and devices. This can be acquired through careful planning and implementation.

Code profiling and optimization techniques

In order to discover performance bottlenecks, enhance efficiency, and optimize the overall performance of their JavaScript code, web developers need to have code profiling and optimization techniques in their arsenal. These techniques are critical tools that any web developer should have by their side. The process of code profiling entails examining the execution of a program in order to locate the sections of the program that are inefficient or perform poorly. Using a variety of profiling tools and methodologies, developers are able to analyze a variety of aspects, including the utilization of the central processing unit (CPU), the consumption of memory, the activity on the network, and the rendering performance. This enables them to zero in on specific portions of their code that may be creating performance issues.

The utilization of browser developer tools, such as Chrome DevTools or Firefox Developer Tools, which come equipped with built-in profiling and performance measurement capabilities, is a frequent method for code profiling. Using these tools, developers are able to collect and evaluate performance data like as CPU utilization, memory allocation, and JavaScript execution time. Additionally, they are able to see the results in real time, which allows them to spot potential bottlenecks and places that may be optimized. In addition, browser developer tools provide features like as flame graphs, call stacks, and timeline recordings. These features offer developers detailed insights into the performance characteristics of JavaScript code and assist developers in diagnosing and fixing performance issues.

Utilizing dedicated profiling libraries and tools, such as the Chrome Performance Analysis Toolkit (Chrome PAT) or the Firefox Profiler, is yet another method that is widely used for code profiling. By providing comprehensive profiling features and in-depth analysis of JavaScript code execution, these tools enable developers to detect hotspots, evaluate function calls, and track memory usage over time. In addition, these tools give additional capabilities. In addition, profiling tools like Stats.js and FPSMeter.js can be utilized to monitor frame rates, frames per second decreases, and rendering performance in real time. This provides developers with the ability to improve animations, transitions, and other visual effects.

Once performance bottlenecks have been found by code profiling, developers are able to employ a variety of optimization approaches in order to increase the efficiency and speed of their JavaScript code. One technique that is frequently used for optimization is called code refactoring. This technique involves reorganizing and rewriting code in order to make it more efficient and accessible for maintenance. The optimization of algorithms, the reduction of the number of function calls, the elimination of superfluous code, and the utilization of data structures and algorithms that are more efficient are few examples of this. Additionally, developers can optimize JavaScript code by minimizing DOM interaction, reducing memory use, and enhancing rendering efficiency by utilizing techniques such as requestAnimationFrame() or CSS transforms. These strategies can be utilized to optimize the performance of rendering.

Another strategy for optimization is called lazy loading, and it involves delaying the loading of resources or code that are not important until they are required. It is possible to enhance performance and reduce the amount of time it takes for a page to load initially by using lazy loading. This technique involves loading resources only when they are required, rather than loading them all at once. Because of this, developers are able to prioritize vital material and defer loading of secondary or less important resources until after the first page load. This is especially advantageous for large or complicated web applications that have a high number of dependencies or resources.

In addition, developers have the ability to enhance the efficiency of their JavaScript code by optimizing network queries and lowering latency. This may include techniques like as bundling and minification, which reduce the size of JavaScript files and improve download times. Additionally, leverage caching tactics to cache static assets and reduce server load. These techniques are examples of techniques that might be included in this category. In addition, developers have the ability to optimize network requests by employing strategies such as prefetching, preloading, and resource hints. These strategies allow developers to prefetch or preload essential resources and reduce latency, thereby enhancing the rate at which pages load and the overall user experience.

Code profiling and optimization techniques are crucial tools for enhancing the performance and efficiency of JavaScript code in web development. In conclusion, these approaches are essential tools. Developers are able to optimize their JavaScript code in order to deliver web applications that are faster, more efficient, and more responsive. This is accomplished by utilizing code profiling tools and techniques to identify performance bottlenecks and by applying optimization techniques such as code refactoring, lazy loading, and network optimization. It is possible for developers to ensure that their JavaScript code satisfies the performance needs of today's users and devices by performing rigorous profiling, analysis, and optimization. This facilitates the creation of a user experience that is both seamless and engaging.

CHAPTER X

Deploying and Maintaining JavaScript Applications

Deployment strategies for JavaScript applications

The deployment techniques for JavaScript applications are essential components of the software development lifecycle. These strategies determine the manner in which applications are packed, delivered, and made accessible to end users. Through the implementation of efficient deployment techniques, the process of releasing updates can be streamlined, transitions between development, staging, and production environments can be made without any interruptions, and the performance and availability of applications can be optimized. Continuous Integration and Continuous Deployment, also referred to as CI/CD is a deployment approach that is frequently used for JavaScript applications. This strategy automates the process of developing, testing, and delivering code changes to production environments. With the assistance of continuous integration and continuous delivery pipelines, developers are able to upload code changes to version control systems like Git, where they are then automatically tested, built, and deployed to production environments without any involvement from a human. By doing so, updates are guaranteed to be distributed in a timely and dependable manner, hence lowering the likelihood of errors and downtime.

Blue-green deployment is an additional deployment technique for JavaScript applications. This deployment approach entails keeping two production environments that are similar to one another, one of which is "blue" and the other of which is "green," and switching between the two environments for each deployment. By doing so, developers are able to publish modifications to one environment while simultaneously maintaining the other environment as a live environment that users can access. Traffic is routed from the old environment to the new environment once the new version has been deployed and tested. This guarantees that consumers have a smooth transition from the past environment to the new environment and helps to limit the amount of downtime that customers experience. A rollback mechanism is also provided by blue-green deployment, which enables developers to immediately revert to the prior version in the event that problems or failures occur.

Additionally, containerization has emerged as a common deployment approach for JavaScript applications. This strategy makes use of technologies such as Docker and Kubernetes to bundle applications and their dependencies into containers that are lightweight and portable. Containers offer programs a runtime environment that is both consistent and isolated, which makes it much simpler to deploy and maintain applications across a variety of infrastructure platforms and settings. Kubernetes and other container orchestration technologies automate the deployment, scaling, and management of containers. Developers are able to deploy and maintain programs in a manner that is both more efficient and dependable as a result of this.

Serverless deployment is another developing deployment technique for JavaScript applications. This strategy makes use of serverless computing platforms like Amazon Web Services Lambda, Google Cloud Functions, and Microsoft Azure Functions to execute code in response to events without the need to make or manage servers. The underlying infrastructure is abstracted away by serverless platforms, which enables developers to concentrate on creating code and delivering applications without having to worry about the provisioning, scaling, or maintenance of servers. This makes it possible for developers to deploy JavaScript applications in a more timely and effective manner, reduce the amount of overhead associated with operations, and dynamically scale applications in response to increases or decreases in demand.

Furthermore, content delivery networks, often known as CDNs, are a frequent deployment strategy for JavaScript applications. These networks allow developers to distribute static assets like HTML, CSS, JavaScript, and images across a network of edge servers that are placed closer to the end users. Through the delivery of material from servers that are physically closer to consumers, content delivery networks (CDNs) cache static assets on edge servers, thereby reducing latency and boosting performance. In addition, content delivery networks (CDNs) offer features such as caching, compression, and network optimization, which further enhance the performance and availability of JavaScript applications.

In conclusion, deployment strategies for JavaScript applications play an essential part in the software development lifecycle. These strategies determine the manner in which programs are packaged, delivered, and made accessible to end users. In order to enhance the performance and availability of applications, effective deployment techniques streamline the process of distributing updates, ensure that transitions between environments are seamless, and ensure that the process is simplified. Using deployment strategies such as Continuous Integration and Continuous Deployment, blue-green deployment, containerization, serverless computing, as well as content delivery networks, developers are able to deploy JavaScript applications in a more efficient, reliable, and scalable manner. This ensures that end users have a user experience that is both seamless and engaging.

Continuous integration and deployment (CI/CD) pipelines

Continuous Integration and Deployment (CI/CD) pipelines have become indispensable tools in modern software development, particularly in the realm of JavaScript applications. These pipelines automate the procedure of integrating code changes, running tests, building artifacts, and deploying applications, resulting in faster delivery cycles, improved code quality, and increased efficiency. In the context of JavaScript applications, CI/CD pipelines streamline the development process by enabling developers to continuously test and deploy code changes, ensuring that updates are delivered quickly and reliably to end users.

The CI/CD pipeline typically begins with the integration phase, where developers push code changes to a version control system such as Git. As soon as code changes are pushed, the CI/CD pipeline automatically triggers a series of automated tests to verify the integrity and functionality of the codebase. These tests may include unit tests, integration tests, end-to-end tests, and performance tests, ensuring that code changes do not introduce regressions or break existing functionality. By running tests automatically and continuously, developers can catch bugs and issues early in the development process, reducing the likelihood of costly errors slipping into production.

Once the code changes have been successfully tested, the CI/CD pipeline moves to the deployment phase, where the code changes are built into deployable artifacts and deployed to production or staging environments. In the case of JavaScript applications, this may involve bundling and minifying JavaScript files, optimizing assets, and generating deployment packages that can be deployed to web servers or cloud platforms. By automating the deployment process, CI/CD pipelines enable developers to release updates quickly and reliably, reducing the time and effort required to deploy changes manually.

One of the main advantages of CI/CD pipelines in JavaScript applications is the ability to enforce code quality and consistency through automated checks and tests. CI/CD pipelines can be configured to enforce coding standards, code formatting rules, and best practices, ensuring that code changes adhere to established guidelines and conventions. Additionally, CI/CD pipelines can perform static code analysis and code reviews, identifying potential issues such as code smells, security vulnerabilities, and performance bottlenecks early in the development process. This helps maintain code quality and consistency across the codebase, making it easier to maintain and scale JavaScript applications over time.

Another benefit of CI/CD pipelines in JavaScript applications is the ability to enable Continuous Deployment, where code changes are automatically deployed to production environments as soon as they pass tests. Continuous Deployment streamlines the release process, allowing developers to release updates to end users quickly and frequently without manual intervention. This enables faster iteration cycles, shorter feedback loops, and more responsive development practices, ultimately leading to faster time-to-market and increased competitiveness in the marketplace.

Furthermore, CI/CD pipelines in JavaScript applications enable developers to implement Continuous Integration practices, where code changes are integrated frequently and continuously into the main codebase. Continuous Integration promotes collaboration and teamwork among developers by ensuring that changes are integrated and tested frequently, reducing integration conflicts and merge headaches. By integrating changes early and often, developers can identify and resolve integration issues quickly, ensuring that the codebase remains stable and healthy throughout the development process.

In conclusion, Continuous Integration and Deployment (CI/CD) pipelines are essential tools for streamlining the development, testing, and deployment of JavaScript applications. By automating the procedure of integrating code changes, running tests, and deploying updates, CI/CD pipelines enable developers to release updates quickly and reliably, ensuring a seamless and efficient development process. With CI/CD pipelines, developers can enforce code quality and consistency, enable Continuous Deployment practices, and promote collaboration and teamwork among development teams, ultimately leading to faster time-to-market as well as increased competitiveness in the marketplace.

Monitoring and maintaining JavaScript applications

In order to guarantee the dependability, performance, and availability of JavaScript applications in production environments, it is vital to monitor and maintain these applications. The use of monitoring tools and methods is becoming progressively important in the identification and resolution of problems, the enhancement of performance, and the provision of a smooth user experience. This is because JavaScript applications are becoming ever more complex and essential to the operations of businesses. Monitoring is the process of tracking a variety of metrics and indicators, including response times, error rates, CPU usage, memory consumption, and network traffic, in order to acquire insights into the health and performance of JavaScript applications.

The process of collecting and analyzing logs and metrics that are generated by JavaScript applications and the infrastructure that supports them is one of the most important components of monitoring JavaScript applications. It is possible for developers to collect and record significant events, failures, and debugging information from JavaScript applications by utilizing logging frameworks such as Log4js, Winston, or Bunyan. It is possible for developers to spot patterns, trends, and anomalies through the analysis of logs and metrics. This allows them to pinpoint potential problems or performance bottlenecks that may have an effect on the user experience. Not only that, but monitoring tools like Datadog, New Relic, and Prometheus offer centralized dashboards and visualizations that collect and display metrics in real time. This makes it possible for developers to monitor the health as well as performance of their applications in a proactive manner.

Implementing alerting and notification systems to notify developers of serious errors or abnormalities is another key part of monitoring JavaScript applications. These mechanisms are known as "notification mechanisms." The configuration of alerting systems like PagerDuty, Slack, or email alerts allows for the activation of notifications in response to the fulfillment of predetermined thresholds or conditions. These conditions may include high error rates, low response times, or server unavailability instances. Developers are able to respond promptly to issues, analyze root causes, and take corrective actions when they receive timely notifications. This helps to reduce downtime and make sure that JavaScript applications are available.

In addition, monitoring JavaScript applications entails keeping track of and managing performance measures like response times, latency, and throughput in order to guarantee the best possible user experience. Using performance monitoring tools like Google Lighthouse, WebPageTest, or GTmetrix, developers are able to assess and optimize many elements of web performance. These characteristics include the amount of time it takes for pages to load, the rendering performance, and the amount of resources that are used. Increasing the perceived speed and responsiveness of JavaScript applications can be accomplished by developers through the monitoring of performance metrics and the optimization of essential rendering paths. This will ultimately result in increased user satisfaction and engagement.

When it comes to JavaScript applications, it is vital to not only monitor performance indicators but also monitor and manage dependencies and interactions with third-party services. Third-party dependencies, which include npm packages, APIs, and external services, have the potential to bring vulnerabilities, stability difficulties, and performance bottlenecks if they are not managed appropriately. The process of discovering and upgrading dependencies that are either obsolete or vulnerable can be automated with the use of dependency monitoring tools such as Snyk, Dependabot, or Greenkeeper. This helps to ensure that JavaScript applications continue to be secure, stable, and up to date.

Additionally, in order to guarantee the applications' stability, scalability, and security, executing regular health checks, load testing, and security audits is an essential part of monitoring JavaScript applications. The purpose of health checks is to ensure that the application's essential components and services are operating appropriately and that they are satisfying the performance standards that have been established beforehand. While performing load testing, it is necessary to simulate user traffic and load on the application in order to detect performance bottlenecks and scalability concerns that may arise under heavy load situations. During security audits, the application code, configuration, and architecture are examined and analyzed in order to detect potential security flaws and weaknesses. These vulnerabilities and weaknesses may include Cross-Site Scripting (XSS), Cross-Site Request Forgery (CSRF), or SQL injection.

In conclusion, monitoring as well as maintaining JavaScript applications are critical activities that must be implemented in order to guarantee the dependability, performance, and availability of these applications in production contexts. Using techniques such as collecting and analyzing logs, metrics, and performance data, putting in place mechanisms for alerting and notification, optimizing performance, managing dependencies, and performing regular health checks and security audits, developers are able to proactively identify as well as address issues, optimize performance, and provide a seamless user experience. It is possible for developers to guarantee that JavaScript applications will continue to be stable, scalable, and secure if they have appropriate monitoring and maintenance methods in place. This will serve to fulfill the requirements and expectations of users and stakeholders.

CONCLUSION

Recap of Key Concepts

When it comes to web development, JavaScript is considered to be one of the most fundamental languages. It is the language that serves as the foundation for dynamic and interactive web sites. It is necessary for any developer who wants to become an expert in web development to have a profound understanding of its fundamental concepts. JavaScript, at its heart, is a versatile scripting language that allows for the development of dynamic content, interacts with users, and manipulates HTML and CSS in order to build web experiences that are engaging. Variables are an essential part of the JavaScript programming language. Variables are used to hold data values and can be modified in many parts of the program. When it comes to making good use of variables, having a solid understanding of data types like strings, numbers, booleans, arrays, and objects is absolutely necessary. In addition, developers are able to manage the flow of execution in their programs through the use of control flow techniques like as conditional statements (if-else), loops (for, while), and switch statements. By acting as reusable pieces of code, functions contribute to the improvement of code organization and the promotion of modularity. The ability to declare functions in JavaScript either in the usual manner or as arrow functions offers a degree of flexibility regarding coding styles.

Within a program, the accessibility of variables and functions is defined by the concept of scope, which is another essential concept. To avoid unexpected variable collisions and to improve the readability of code, it is important to have a solid understanding of the distinction between global and local scope. The utilization of classes and objects is another way in which JavaScript is able to assist object-oriented programming. In contrast to classes, which act as blueprints for the creation of objects with shared attributes and methods, objects are responsible for encapsulating both data and activity. Prototypes are an essential component of the inheritance model in JavaScript. They make it possible for objects to inherit properties and methods from other objects via inheritance. The use of techniques such as callbacks, promises, and async/await are examples of asynchronous programming techniques that enable non-blocking execution. This approach is another crucial component. For the purpose of performing tasks such as retrieving data from servers or carrying out processes that take a significant amount of time without causing the user interface to become frozen, asynchronous actions are essential.

It is possible for JavaScript to dynamically change HTML components through the use of the Document Object Model (DOM), which depicts the structure of HTML documents as a tree-like hierarchy of objects. When it comes to establishing interactive web pages and improving user experiences, having a solid understanding of DOM manipulation techniques is absolutely necessary. The ability to respond to user events, including as clicks, mouse movements, and keyboard inputs, is made possible for developers by virtue of event handling. It is possible for developers to execute JavaScript code in response to certain events by adding event listeners to HTML elements. This makes it possible for online applications to be interactive. In addition, JavaScript provides an array of built-in methods and functions that facilitate the efficient manipulation of data structures such as arrays, strings, and other data structures. Regular expressions are a powerful tool that contributes to the sophisticated data processing capabilities of JavaScript.

These expressions can be used to match patterns and manipulate text.

Error management is an essential component of JavaScript development. It ensures that runtime failures are handled in a smooth manner, which helps to prevent program crashes and improves the user experience. The use of try-catch blocks enables developers to handle exceptions in a smooth manner and build fallback mechanisms in the event that errors occur. Debugging tools, which are made available by contemporary web browsers and integrated development environments (IDEs), make it easier to locate as well as fix errors in code, which in turn improves the workflow of the development process. When it comes to avoiding typical security vulnerabilities, such as cross-site scripting (XSS) and injection attacks, having a solid understanding of the principles underlying secure coding standards is absolutely necessary. It is possible for developers to protect their online applications from potential dangers by validating the data that is input, sanitizing the inputs that users provide, and putting in place the appropriate authentication and authorization systems.

In conclusion, JavaScript basics include a wide variety of theoretical frameworks and practical approaches that are necessary for the development of contemporary web applications. For developers, having a firm grasp on these foundations gives them the ability to create online experiences that are dynamic, interactive, and safe. Developers are able to construct JavaScript programs that are both reliable and effective if they have a profound understanding of fundamental concepts such as variables, data types, control flow, functions, scope, object-oriented programming, asynchronous programming, DOM manipulation, event management, and error handling. By consistently improving these abilities through practice, experimenting, and staying up to date with industry trends, developers may ensure that they continue to be proficient in JavaScript programming and capable of solving complicated challenges in the always shifting web ecosystem.

Final Thoughts on JavaScript Essentials

As we conclude our exploration of JavaScript essentials, it's evident that this programming language stands as a cornerstone of modern web development. JavaScript's versatility, flexibility, and ubiquity make it an indispensable tool for developers worldwide. Throughout our journey, we've delved into key concepts that form the foundation of JavaScript proficiency, empowering developers to establish dynamic and interactive web experiences. From variables and data types to control flow mechanisms and functions, understanding these fundamentals is essential for harnessing JavaScript's full potential. Moreover, mastering concepts like scope, object-oriented programming, and asynchronous programming equips developers with the skills to build scalable and efficient applications.

The Document Object Model (DOM) serves as a gateway for JavaScript to manipulate HTML elements dynamically, enabling developers to create responsive and engaging user interfaces. By mastering DOM manipulation techniques and event handling, developers can craft web applications that respond intuitively to user interactions. Furthermore, JavaScript's built-in methods and functions for data manipulation and regular expressions provide powerful tools for processing and transforming data efficiently. Understanding error handling principles and secure coding practices is paramount for ensuring the reliability and security of JavaScript applications, safeguarding against potential vulnerabilities and threats.

Looking ahead, JavaScript continues to evolve rapidly, driven by innovations in web technologies and emerging trends in software development. As the boundaries between front-end and back-end development blur with the rise of full-stack JavaScript frameworks like Node.js, developers are presented with new opportunities to leverage their JavaScript skills across the entire software stack. Additionally, the growing popularity of progressive web apps (PWAs) and serverless architectures underscores JavaScript's relevance in building modern, scalable, and resilient web applications.

Beyond technical proficiency, cultivating a growth mindset and a passion for learning is essential for staying abreast of JavaScript's ever-changing landscape. Engaging with the vibrant JavaScript community through forums, meetups, and online communities fosters collaboration, knowledge sharing, and continuous improvement. Embracing best practices like code reviews, automated testing, and continuous integration/continuous deployment (CI/CD) pipelines enhances code quality and accelerates the development lifecycle.

In conclusion, JavaScript essentials encompass not only a set of technical concepts but also a mindset of adaptability, curiosity, and collaboration. By mastering the fundamentals of JavaScript and staying attuned to industry trends and best practices, developers can embark on a fulfilling journey of innovation and creativity in web development. As JavaScript continues to shape the digital landscape, the possibilities for innovation are limitless, and the opportunities for developers are boundless. With a solid foundation in JavaScript essentials and a commitment to lifelong learning, developers are poised to thrive in the dynamic and ever-evolving world of web development.

Resources for Further Learning

As you embark on your journey to master JavaScript essentials, it's essential to have access to a diverse array of resources that cater to various learning styles and skill levels. Fortunately, the wealth of resources available both online and offline makes it easier than ever to deepen your understanding of JavaScript and hone your programming skills. For beginners, interactive online platforms like Codecademy, freeCodeCamp, and Khan Academy offer introductory courses that cover the basics of JavaScript syntax, data types, control flow, and functions. These platforms provide hands-on coding exercises and projects, allowing learners to hone their skills in a supportive environment.

For those desiring a more structured approach to learning JavaScript, online courses offered by platforms like Udemy, Coursera, and Pluralsight provide comprehensive curricula taught by industry experts. These courses typically cover an array of topics, including advanced JavaScript concepts, DOM manipulation, asynchronous programming, and modern frameworks/libraries like React, Angular, and Vue.js. Additionally, many of these platforms offer certification programs that can enhance your credentials and credibility as a JavaScript developer.

Books remain a valuable resource for delving deeper into JavaScript concepts and gaining a more comprehensive understanding of the language. Classic texts like "Eloquent JavaScript" by Marijn Haverbeke, "JavaScript: The Good Parts" by Douglas Crockford, and "You Don't Know JS" series by Kyle Simpson are widely regarded as must-reads for aspiring JavaScript developers. These books provide in-depth explanations, code examples, and best practices for writing clean, efficient, as well as maintainable JavaScript code.

Online tutorials and blogs are another invaluable resource for staying updated on the latest JavaScript trends, techniques, and best practices. Websites like MDN Web Docs, JavaScript.info, and CSS-Tricks offer comprehensive documentation, tutorials, and articles covering a wide range of JavaScript topics. Following prominent JavaScript bloggers and developers on platforms like Medium, Dev.to, and Twitter can also provide valuable insights, tips, and tutorials from seasoned professionals in the field.

Engaging with the JavaScript community through forums, discussion groups, and online communities is an excellent way to seek help, share knowledge, and also collaborate with fellow developers. Platforms like Stack Overflow, Reddit's r/javascript community, and Discord servers dedicated to JavaScript provide forums for asking questions, troubleshooting issues, and participating in discussions about JavaScript-related topics. Attending local meetups, workshops, and conferences focused on JavaScript and web development can also provide valuable networking opportunities and hands-on learning experiences.

Lastly, experimenting with personal projects and contributing to open-source projects on platforms like GitHub is a fantastic way to apply your JavaScript skills in real-world scenarios and collaborate with other developers. Building your portfolio of projects not only showcases your expertise but also allows you to learn from practical experience and feedback from peers and mentors.

In conclusion, the abundance of resources available for learning JavaScript essentials empowers aspiring developers to embark on a journey of continuous growth as well as improvement. Whether you prefer interactive online platforms, structured courses, books, tutorials, community forums, or hands-on projects, there's a wealth of resources to suit your learning style and preferences. By leveraging these resources effectively and embracing a mindset of lifelong learning and curiosity, you can unlock the full potential of JavaScript and propel your career as a proficient and versatile developer in the ever-evolving world of web development.

Thank you for buying and reading/listening to our book. If you found this book useful/helpful please take a few minutes and leave a review on the platform where you purchased our book. Your feedback matters greatly to us.